BLACK BEHIND THE SHIELD

BLACK BEHIND THE SHIELD

A COLLECTION OF STORIES THE WORLD NEEDS TO HEAR

Matthew Barnwell III

Copyright © 2020 by Matthew Barnwell III

All rights reserved. This book or any portions thereof may not be reproduced or used in any matter whatsoever without express written permission of the publisher, except by a reviewer who may quote brief passages in a review to be printed in a newspaper, magazine, or journal.

Disclaimer: This is a work of creative non-fiction. The events and experiences covered herein have been faithfully remembered by the author to the best of his abilities and are all true. Some of the names and other details have been changed to protect the privacy of the individuals involved.

ISBN#: 979-8-218-03797-0
Imprint: Independently published
ShieldMB3, LLC

Cover design: Erin Ortega/erinortega@me.com

Printed in the United States of America

blackbehindtheshield@outlook.com

In dedication to you Mom
"...ten fingers and ten toes"

AUTHOR'S NOTE

I knew as a young Black kid that I wanted to be a police officer. Growing up in NYC directly and indirectly groomed me to walk down that path. I was fortunate enough to have been able to spend over 24 years of my life as a Connecticut State Trooper, in my opinion one of the best agencies in the country. Some of those years were great and some I wanted to leave in the rearview, but all of them were as a man of color.

At the time, I didn't realize how difficult it would be to be a State Trooper. Being a Black trooper, especially in such an overwhelmingly white state as Connecticut, added a whole new element to the job that I would find out later would be a detriment, but also a blessing. I've been involved in things I wouldn't wish on my worst enemy, but there have also been episodes and events that made me eternally proud.

The stories I'm about to share with you are as I remember them. Some, I haven't told to anyone before. This is how it all began...

PREFACE

I was conducting surveillance on this high-level drug bust. We had two bad guys in our sights when my name came over the police radio. It was unexpected so there was a little pucker factor happening, but I kept my cool and listened. It was one of my sergeants who was requesting—well, more like telling me on the radio— to go into the supermarket, blend in, and keep an eye on the second guy.

My initial thought was, "Are you crazy?"

It wasn't that I didn't want to do it, it just didn't make sense. Yes, he was Black, but in two hours I hadn't seen one person of color exit or enter that supermarket and I'm quite sure the other detectives and police personnel saw the same thing, so why not send a white officer inside? I was pretty sure he or she would have had a better chance of blending in than I would.

This was a perfect case of "Because you're Black and he's Black." But it wasn't my operation nor was it my decision, so I said, "Roger" into the radio and did what I was told.

I got out of my car with nothing more than my gun in my waistband and a baseball cap with the word "police" on it. I put the cap on backwards so that if the second suspect saw me all he would see was a backwards baseball cap.

I started to walk towards the front door of the supermarket and just as I was about to go in, there was a loud screeching of cars. I quickly turned toward the parking lot.

Cops were jumping out of cars and vans and running towards me.

One detective ran past yelling "Go get the second guy!"

I drew my gun and entered the store along with a bunch of other detectives and officers.

The place was flooded with police. It was like a scene from a movie. Cops ran up and down aisles with their guns out. Customers fell to the ground with their hands over their faces in fear. There were even customers jumping behind the butcher's counter, dragging other customers with them. It was crazy.

I walked through the supermarket carefully, my police cap on backwards and my gun in my hand. Someone said the second guy was towards the rear down an aisle close to the other end.

I moved briskly toward that aisle. As I got there I slowed and began to walk from the front of the aisle toward the rear, my gun pointing at the ground. I was like a cat about to pounce on a mouse.

I reached the end of the aisle and scanned the rear of the store, hoping to spot the second guy.

A voice boomed from behind me: "DROP YOUR GUN OR I'LL DROP YOU!"

I was the only one in that aisle holding a gun. The voice was distinct. It was a voice I knew.

I'm not sure if it was the city in me or just my common sense, but I knew enough not to make any sudden moves.

I put my hands up, one of which was holding my gun, and was able to turn my head without moving my body. I looked over my shoulder and saw another cop, "Joe," pointing his gun right at my head.

This was Joe, the same guy who didn't want to help me when I got to the office a few months before this moment. The same Joe who I'd since worked with every day and who was at the briefing for this operation just a few hours ago. The same guy I entered the supermarket with a few seconds ago for God's sakes! So, I did the only thing I could do. I yelled back at him.

"Joe it's Matt! Don't shoot me!"

There was a pause and then Joe recognized me. He lowered his gun. "Oh, shit dude, my bad."

All the cops in the supermarket raced over to the aisle I was in.

"Matt where's the guy?" someone asked me.

"Joe thought I was the guy," I said, not able to hide the disgust in my voice.

The other detectives who were in my office couldn't believe Joe had made that mistake. Some showed their displeasure. Some showed it verbally and some showed it physically.

Meanwhile, the suspect had somehow slipped away.

We caught a break a few hours later when he was captured trying to hitchhike back to New York, but it should've never gotten that far. He should've never gotten away from the supermarket. All because one of my co-workers couldn't—or wouldn't—remember my Black face. I guess we all looked the same to him.

Welcome to my life of more than 24 years of being Black behind the shield.

Chapter 1
THE BEGINNING

It was the early 1970's and Christmas time in New York City. My favorite time of the year. I was six and my little sister was five. When my family and I would walk through our neighborhood we'd smell the pine Christmas trees lined up on the sidewalk being sold by the vendors.

Every year I couldn't wait for Christmas to come. My sister and I would wake up at the crack of dawn on Christmas Day with our eyes filled with excitement.

It never mattered to us what we got as long as we were all together. We both couldn't be happier and didn't have a care in the world. But for us not to have a care in the world our parents had to endure the time prior to the 70's.

I didn't realize when I was young how important the 1960's were for my parents, as well as American History. The Civil Rights Act of 1964 was passed, Martin Luther King Jr. was leading the country in a fight for equality when he was assassinated in 1968, and in the midst of it all, I was born. I learned these things had to happen so my sister and I could enjoy our Christmases together, free and without worry.

My story began in the summer of 1966, in one of the most notable and recognizable cities in the world: New York, specifically Harlem. The day I was born was one of the hottest days in the city. It's hard for me to forget that, as my mother likes to remind me every year of the record heat wave she endured bringing me into this world. She only jokes about how troublesome I was. From the beginning she knew how to lead me through life and into my own important years.

My mother, Marilyn, is one of the kindest souls you'll ever meet. She's a teacher and has always been nurturing. She took the time to teach us about life and what to expect when we got older. As a mother, she never missed a beat, especially if we did something wrong. She'd make sure we saw the wrong in our ways and helped us learn from our mistakes.

She was the one who looked me directly in the eyes and told me, "You can be whatever you want to be."

When you're black and young, that's the last thing you believe.

I tried to test her. "There's no way I could be President."

Without blinking an eye, she said to me, "If that's what you want to be, then of course you can."

My father, Matthew Jr., was a grammar-school principal. He was very strict. To put it plainly, he was old school. He had a "Do as I say" mentality. It seemed harsh sometimes, but we knew it was out of love and to keep our family safe. His strict ways allowed me to become thicker skinned, which would ultimately help prepare me for my career in law enforcement.

Growing up in Harlem, when you got in trouble you didn't get the luxury of a time out. Instead, you heard, "Go get me the belt." Whenever my sister or I heard those words, we knew it was game over. One thing was for sure though, after getting the belt, you can bet I didn't make the same mistake again. He loved my sister and me with everything he had and I'm proud to say he helped make me the man I am today.

My sister, Michele, is only 15 months younger than me, which means we spent our entire childhood bothering one another. As an older brother, it was my job to antagonize her, but I was the only one allowed to do it. Growing up she often asked me for advice. Once when she was about four, she came to me and asked me how to spell the word "pizza." I happily obliged and began to spell it for her, "A-B-C, D…" all the way to the letter Z.

Excited to have learned a new word, she ran to show our mom her hard work.

Mom saw her lengthy spelling of the word "pizza."

"Michele, where did you learn this?"

"From Matthew!" she exclaimed.

I was quickly fired from my position as her teacher.

We often argued, but deep down it was nothing but love. She drove me crazy, and while I'm hesitant to admit it, I know I drove her crazy too. Regardless of what happened, I always had her back and that remains true to this day.

In addition to my own sibling, I was lucky enough to grow up in a time where every kid who lived in your building, or on your block, was like your brother or sister. It was one giant family, but with fewer mouths to feed. The adults acted as extra parents to all us kids, so if you acted up, there was a good chance they would scold you as they would their own. Even though they only knew you because you played tag or rode your skateboard in front of their building.

The superintendent, or the super, as we called him, ran our building and ensured everything worked as it should. He walked around with a constant frown and a cigar that seemed to live between his lips. Behind his scary demeanor, however, he had a soft spot for all of us. I thought I might have crossed a line one day when my rock-throwing adventures resulted in a broken light bulb... inside the building. As soon as it happened, my stomach dropped. I felt like a dead kid walking. He didn't get mad though, instead he taught me to be honest and take responsibility for my actions. The super and that collection of building parents made sure to take good care of me, but nothing superseded the support and love I got from my very own family.

Growing up in Harlem had its advantages. I never stood out because everyone looked like me. At that time, if you weren't a person of color in Harlem *you* were the minority. When something went bad, everyone in the neighborhood had your back even if they barely knew you. Contrary to popular belief, one could feel pretty safe being out at night in Harlem, at least I did. I was young, so I didn't worry about much. My family and my older friends made sure that I was kept away from the "bad" crowd and because of that I felt I could do anything. They made me feel there was nowhere I'd rather be, and I knew I could always count on them if I needed to. Besides I learned at a very young age that if you don't need to be somewhere, then don't go there.

Black Behind the Shield

I was an inquisitive kid. I paid attention to the things and the people around me. I'd ask why something, or someone, was the way it was. I watched the way people walked and listened to them talk. Maybe because I was nosey, I started to understand people, to read them and their mannerisms and their reasons for doing certain things. Harlem provided me with an unlimited resource when it came to people. My "nosiness" would become an asset as I got older. To this day I feel blessed and proud to have grown up where I did.

My family and I lived in a six-story apartment building that was constructed of old, weathered brick and came equipped with an empty lot in the rear that bordered a few other apartment buildings. Many of the residents decided they were too lazy to properly dispose of their trash, so that empty lot served more as a landing pad for the full garbage bags people would drop from their windows. There was always a terrible stench emitting from our makeshift dumping grounds. It was worse than spoiled eggs that had been left in the sun for three weeks. We learned to live with this putrid smell. There was no other option.

As a kid, I used to stare out the kitchen window and see how many rats I could count in the garbage-ridden lot below. I often mistook them for cats because I was watching from six stories up. It never bothered me. It was all I knew. Back then, that was city living and I enjoyed every minute of it.

Our building was set in the middle of a steep New York City hill. The sidewalks were grimy and scattered with broken bottles left behind by the neighborhood drunks. The hill was also the perfect place for skateboarding. It was a pivotal part of my youth. I would fly down, whizzing by my mom, who I'm sure had a heart attack every time she saw me.

Every so often she'd send me to the store at the top of the hill and bet that she could count to 10 before I returned. I was always determined to prove her wrong, so I'd burst through the door and barrel up the street like a dog chasing a rabbit. A short while later, I'd burst back through the door, package in hand, sweating and out of breath from my race against the clock. Every time I returned; she'd only have reached the number nine. I remained victorious, or so I thought. I later learned she wasn't actually counting. She'd wait until she heard me at the door to exclaim, she'd only reached nine. She, in her own sneaky way, was looking out for me. The quicker I got back, the less time I spent in harm's way.

Chapter 2
MY BIKE

In my early years there were three things I wanted to be when I grew up. The first was a singer. People who know me know I can't sing to save my life but put me in a shower and I'm a regular Luther Vandross.

The second was an actor. As kids growing up in Harlem my friends and I had dreams, hopes and aspirations about being on the big screen, but never did we think they were actually attainable. We daydreamed about it for a little while, then we came back to reality. I still have that desire for acting. I don't think I'll ever give that up.

The third was a police officer. It seemed the easiest out of the three to become, and as a kid I was all about the easy way out.

A lot of games we played centered around or involved some version of cops and robbers. I hated being the robber. Somehow, I always ended up on the ground with my face attached to the pavement. Even at a young age playing those games it was evident that the bad guy always ended up on the ground. I'm not sure if it was TV or just the streets, but that's what we were conditioned to believe. I didn't realize how badly I wanted to become a police officer until an incident with my bike helped ignite that feeling of one day wearing the shield.

Most kids in my neighborhood had bikes. Some were top of the line, and some looked like they were put together with duct tape. Seriously, many a bike rocked various colors of duct tape. The bike was our preferred means of transportation, so we were happy with what we had.

We would ride our bikes all day until our legs felt like jelly or wet noodles. Tired wasn't even in our vocabulary. I'd go outside in the morning and sometimes wouldn't come home until the streetlights started to flicker. When those streetlights came all the way on, I'd better be inside my apartment. If I wasn't, I risked meeting my nemesis, "the belt."

My uncle had this saying that would always come to mind at times like this, "Imma set fire to your keister."

That hill I told you about in front of my building became my own personal bike ramp. I'd ride down that hill so fast that the brakes on my bike started to smell like burnt rubber. I didn't need a lot of things to keep me occupied, and that hill was my go-to form of entertainment. My bike was an Apollo 3-speed with a banana seat. Talk about someone being cool, you couldn't tell me anything. I thought I was the coolest kid on the block. It was black and had a bell attached to the handlebars. Most kids always had one toy or possession that was their favorite. Mine was that bike.

My mom always told me to take care of the things I liked so they'd last a long time. One way to keep my bike a long time was to stay in front of our building so when she looked out of our window, she could see me. My mom would explain that if I rode my bike around the corner then I'd be out of her sight, so if something happened, she wouldn't know about it until it was too late.

As young city kids we were oblivious to the outside dangers that exist every day. We were comfortable with our surroundings. I was a good kid, but hard-headed. I'd look my mother right in the face and say, "Yep, I understand," which translated to "Are you done so I can go out and play?" I had selective hearing and that would sometimes bite me directly in my hind parts. I thought: what do I have to worry about?

There were tons of kids playing on my block at any given time. Most of them were older than me. So, I didn't have to worry, cuz' I had peoples!

One summer afternoon, when the sun was at its peak, a bunch of "my peoples" were hanging outside on the block. Some of the girls were playing hopscotch, or whatever it was that kept them out of our hair, and the boys were either playing tag or some other made-up game to keep them occupied.

Then there was me, riding my Apollo 3-speed with that badass banana seat. Saying it out loud now doesn't make me feel it was all that badass.

There had to be at least 10 to 15 of us out there, and we lived on a concrete ski slope. What kind of kid would I be if I didn't take my bike to the top of that slope and come down as fast as humanly possible? There was one problem with that line of thinking: I'd be coming down so fast that once I got to the bottom I had only about 30 yards to stop, or I'd end up in the middle of traffic on Riverside Drive.

Being road pizza was not in my plans. I had no fear growing up, so flying down on my bike and having to stop quickly was a walk in the park. I'd done it so many times it wasn't a big thing.

There I was flying down the hill with the wind slapping me in the face so hard tears were coming from my eyes. I got to the bottom of the hill and for some stupid reason I tried to pedal and almost lost my balance, so I hit the brakes. I wasn't going to be able to stop quick enough so I did what anyone else would've done: I coasted around the corner. It was better than ending up under someone's Dodge station wagon.

Once I was able to control my bike, I made a U-turn so I could head back to the front of my building where all my friends were.

It ended up being the longest U-turn I ever made.

As I turned my bike around and started to pedal back, two older kids who weren't from my neighborhood jumped out in front of me.

I tried to go around them, but they weren't having it. They both stood right in front of me so I couldn't pedal or move anywhere. I'd never been in this type of situation before, and I knew it wasn't good. I said to myself I have three options: 1) try to pedal away, but that would've resulted in me going nowhere; 2) punch one and then try to pedal away, which would've resulted in me getting my ass kicked and still not being able to go anywhere; or 3) just sit there and see what they had to say.

Option three seemed to give me the best chance to keep my teeth in my mouth, so I sat there.

Black Behind the Shield

They both started to laugh. One said, "Hey little man can I have a ride?"

Not being quick-witted at the time and scared shitless, the only thing that I could think to say was, "My mom told me I can't let anyone ride my bike."

Really Matt, that's all you could think of to say?

He said, "If you don't give us a ride, we're just gonna take it."

It quickly became apparent that this could be the last time I'd see my Apollo 3-speed with the banana seat. They both jumped on my bike and took off laughing.

I stood on the sidewalk in shock. I had to figure out what I was going to say when I walked back around the corner without my bike. Since I was around the corner my mother couldn't see me and couldn't do anything to help. I'd heard that before, but my brick-for-a-head self hadn't listened.

I came back crying like I'd been whooped for an hour straight. Maybe I was preparing myself for the real thing. The older kids saw me crying and knew immediately what happened since I was walking and not riding my bike. Three of them looked at each other and then ran off to see if they could find the two kids who took my bike. There was a part of me that wanted them to find them because I wanted my bike back, but another part of me was afraid of what they'd do to those kids if they did find them. But really, I had other things on my mind. One of which was what lie was I going to tell so I didn't get in trouble.

I walked up six flights of stairs instead of taking the elevator in the hopes of prolonging my fate, thinking that was somehow going to help. It didn't.

My mind was ready to lie but my face and mouth didn't get the memo. I told my mother, "You see, what had happened was…" and I stood there waiting for the repercussions. To my surprise all she said was, "Are you ok?"

I thought it might be some sort of trick, but she was more concerned about me than about my bike or my going around the corner. She gave me a hug, then picked up the phone and called the police. In my head I was like, *Hold up, the police? I got my bike stolen; I didn't rob a bank.* I was terrified. I didn't want the police to come. I didn't know if I'd be the one getting in trouble.

My mom and I made our way downstairs and waited for the police to arrive. It was the longest few minutes of my short life, but there was nothing I could do.

A little while later a blue and white squad car with the letters "NYPD" tattooed on the side pulled up in front of our building. When it stopped, two white police officers were inside. All my friends were looking at me as if I were going to jail or something. I was stuck to my mother's hip simply out of fear. I didn't want the police to take me.

My mom explained what happened, and they asked us to get in their squad car so that we could drive around to see if I could spot my bike or the two thieves. I was like, *Hell No!* in my head. I never wanted to see those guys again.

Against my wishes we got in the back seat of their squad car. I felt like nothing short of a criminal. I was so mortified I couldn't care less if I found my bike.

Every few minutes one of the officers would ask me if I saw the kids or my bike. I kept responding no. It was hard to see out the window when the only thing looking out the window was the top of my Afro.

Looking at the backs of the heads of these two white police officers, I thought for sure they were waiting for the right moment to lock me up. All I wanted to do was get out and go home like the day never happened.

I got my wish. They drove us back to the front of my building and after a brief conversation with my mom they took off.

I went upstairs and didn't come back out for the rest of the day. I was scared, but I was also embarrassed.

Later that evening I was watching TV and still sulking about the loss of my bike when the downstairs buzzer rang. Mom asked who it was and the person on the other end said, "It's the police."

Ok, that's it. I was ready to start packing my toothbrush, my Archie comic books and some clothes. I was convinced they'd come back for me.

My mom buzzed them in. I was scared all over again. There was a knock at the door. I was like, *For the love of God please don't answer that,* but I guess she couldn't read my mind. When she opened the door, there they were, the same two white cops from earlier.

I stood behind my mom while she talked to them so I couldn't see much, but I could hear just fine. One of the cops said, "Good evening." What I heard next blew me away.

One of the officers told my mother that after they'd left us, they continued to look for my bike. They were unsuccessful, but they went on a call where they noticed what appeared to be an abandoned bike. They asked the gentleman who I guess owned the bike what he was going to do with it, and he told the two officers he was going to get rid of it. They asked if it would be okay if they took it so they could give it to a kid whose bike had been stolen earlier in the day.

I stood behind my mother taking this all in and thinking I knew a kid this exact same thing happened to—me!

My mom opened the door a little wider and there it was—an old beat-up bike with duct tape around the seat. A banana seat I might add. It only had one speed, and that was forward. It was the ugliest bike I'd ever seen, but it was beautiful. I looked at my mom and asked her if I could keep it. She smiled and said, "Of course!"

I looked at the two white police officers and with a big-ass grin I said, "Thank you!"

That was one of the best days I'd ever had as a kid. To receive a gift like that from two white cops who, for all intents and purposes I thought didn't like Black people, was something unexpected and surreal.

The look of surprise on my mother's face spoke volumes. This wasn't something cops did, at least in our eyes. But their actions changed this little Black kid's version of what a police officer was. I knew then that not all cops were bad.

Black Behind the Shield

That moment confirmed in my heart what I was going to be when I grew up. I wanted to be able to bring that same excitement and joy that I was feeling to someone else.

Still, a thought troubled me: when I was in that police car driving around looking for my bike, why was I scared? That's the last place a young kid should've been scared, Black or not. They weren't the bad guys, but that was my perception. I should've been asking the officers if I could wear their hat or sound the siren a few times. Instead, I was scared and intimidated.

No child should ever fear the police. Unfortunately, there are some officers who give you no choice but to feel that way because of their inability to communicate and empathize with people.

It was a shame that I possessed those feelings. I knew then that my mission was to change those feelings, not only for myself but for others who had similar feelings about the police. It didn't make a difference that they were white, and I was Black. The only thing that mattered was that they helped me when they didn't have to.

The actions of those two officers changed me as a person. The power of that realization remains with me to this very day.

Chapter 3
MY NEW HOOD

My dad was a principal at a public elementary school—or grammar school, as we called it—in the South Bronx. It wasn't the safest place to teach. The South Bronx at that time felt like a war zone. It was made up mostly of Blacks and Hispanics.

When I was in 3rd grade, I'd occasionally go with him while he supervised summer school. Most of the kids there ranged between 5th and 8th grade. You would've thought the regular school year continued into the summer because of the number of kids who were there. From what I saw, none of those kids were going to graduate.

My father patrolled the stuffy classrooms and long hallways, barking at students with his giant megaphone. His bald head and moustache were his signature look, and he acted as if he were in the movie *Lean on Me* and had channeled his inner Morgan Freeman (even though the movie would be released many years later).

Being there was unsettling for a third grader, but sometimes I didn't have a choice. If my father said I was going with him to school, then with him I went.

Keeping a controlled environment during summer school was no easy task, especially with those hellish students who behaved more like a pack of wild animals than actual school children. I once watched an 8th grade girl knock out another girl with one punch, all because she stepped on her sneakers. I made a conscious effort to stay out of her way. One wrong move and I might get knocked out too. I hoped I wouldn't since I was the principal's kid.

I often hung out in my dad's office. His office was spacious with a large oak desk that seemed fit for a king. There wasn't much for a third grader to do during summer school. I'd play with the same old toys I brought from home. When I got bored, I'd roam the halls to see what the rest of the school was up to, keeping in mind what that 8th grader did over a pair of sneakers.

One day I asked my dad if the parents were just as crazy as their children. He noted that some of them tended to get a little out of control, but he said he handled it.

I wasn't quite sure what he was talking about, so I asked him. "How do you handle it?"

He sat calmly in his large leather chair, shrugged his shoulders, and simply stated, "I can handle it."

He was a man of few words, but he gave the impression that, if necessary, he was well equipped to resolve any situation he was thrown into.

To further prove his point, he revealed a wooden baseball bat that he had hidden on his lap. Before I could ask where the bat came from, he turned to open a closet door adjacent to his desk. My eyes almost fell out of my head. In it were all the weapons he'd seized from those wild-ass school kids. He had knives, bats, and other homemade-type weapons. It looked like he could supply a small army.

It made me think about the danger the students posed not only to one another but to the teachers as well as my dad. When he showed me his confiscated arsenal, all I could think of is what would happen if the police knew what he had hidden in his closet. It was the first time in my young life that I was scared not only for him, but for myself. If the police found out they might take him away. And if that happened, what would I do without my father?

I never spoke about what I saw in that closet that day. I didn't want my father to get in trouble.

That was the first time I thought to myself that if I were a police officer, I'd be able to protect him. He wasn't a man to be messed with, nor did he need protection, but if something were to happen, I wanted to be by his side.

My school was quite different from my dad's school. I went to Corpus Christi, a catholic grammar school in lower Harlem. While predominately white, there was a mixture of kids from all different backgrounds. We had mostly nuns and monsignors as teachers. Sister Mary Tyler was my favorite, God rest her soul. It was there I realized that even though people looked different from me, we were very much the same.

The school was located downtown on West 121st St., and to get there I had to take the public bus. There were two other kids in my building who went to school with me, so we'd all take the bus together. We did everything together. We walked to the bus stop together and came home together. We'd leave our building at the same time every day and the same bus driver would be there waiting to pick us up. If we ever ran late, the bus driver would stop in the middle of the road to block traffic so that we could cross the street safely and still make the bus. That's not the case anymore. Nowadays if you're late, you'd better call an Uber.

Our parents ended up separating when I was in 6th grade. My mother, sister and I moved to the Upper West Side of Manhattan, close to Columbia University.

Moving from Harlem to the Upper West Side was a tough time for all of us, but especially for my mom. However, she knew it was something that had to be done, and while I didn't understand it at the time, I trusted that my mom was doing what was best for us. She made a tough situation easier. For that, my sister and I were and still are eternally grateful. She made sacrifices most people wouldn't, and that's why my sister and I are the people we are today.

Leaving my dad was tough for me because he was the male figure I most looked up to, but the move would end up creating the very situation that kick-started something inside of me. This resulted in me becoming a better human being. As my mom always taught us, "Everything happens for a reason." Because of my mom's strength and dedication to our family, that reason soon became clear to me.

I knew the minute we left I'd have to grow up quick. I've never said this to my mom or my sister until right now, but I felt I had to become the man of the house. Not because I wanted to. I had to. My job went from being a kid who had no worries to someone who had to become a protector. The well-being of my mom and sister became job one. I welcomed that job with open arms.

I'm not sure what I would've done if someone had tried to harm either one of them, but I would've done whatever I had to do, even if that meant getting my ass kicked. Nothing's changed. That's still my job today whether they like it or not, whether we're near or far. I will protect them at any time, at any cost, and for any reason.

There was an incident when we were living on the Upper West Side when my sister, then 12, was babysitting our cousin who was about two years old. My sister and our cousin, who was in his stroller, had just returned to our apartment. As my sister was about to enter, a white guy, unknown to any of us, exited our apartment and walked right by her. That's right, my sister interrupted a burglary in progress at our own crib.

This could've been bad in so many ways but my sister, who could think on her feet like nobody's business, calmly asked this guy for the time. He was probably so dumbfounded that this young girl had the gall to say something to him that he stopped and gave her the time before making his escape. He left without taking anything or harming anyone.

I'm not sure there are many 12-year-olds, let alone adults, who would've reacted like she did or had the wherewithal to come up with a ruse to have him stop so that she could at the very least give a good description of him.

When I got home and heard what happened I became enraged. Someone could have hurt members of my family. I went into my room and grabbed one of my many baseball bats in case this guy was still in the area. I was only 13 and I wasn't sure what I would've done if I'd found him, but what I did know was that I was old enough to do whatever I had to do to make sure he never stepped foot in our apartment again.

In a weird way I felt I'd let my sister down. I wasn't there to protect her. I vowed never to let that happen again.

Her actions that day taught me that it's important to stay calm in a stressful situation. Those actions of hers would become more relevant later in my life.

Our move, and that incident involving my sister, indirectly helped make me a protector of not just my family but of other people. I've always tried to help those who couldn't help themselves, even if the odds were against me and danger was imminent. Regardless, I did what I had to do.

These incidents also prepared me to be a more empathetic State Trooper. I looked at situations like domestics differently. I always sided with the victim, whether it was the woman or the man. I felt it was my job to protect them, not because I was a trooper, but because I was a human being. One would think that siding with the victim is a no-brainer, but I've witnessed other cops say, "She (or he) must've deserved it."

There are some women who treat men like punching bags because they think they can get away with it, and I feel for those guys, but I'm from the school that says you don't put your hands on a woman, period.

I've been slapped before, by a female in college, in front of 100-plus people at a party. Unbeknownst to me she liked me. I guess me ignoring her made her feel like I was dissing her. When she slapped me, I got pissed, and felt like knocking her ass into next week, Instead I took it out on the nearest wall I could find.

As a guy—as a man—I believe there are some things you just have to deal with. Like a cop has to deal with verbal abuse from the public. If you act on emotion, like some police officers do, people get hurt. Some cops act on emotion instead of understanding and analyzing each situation and each person, and when they do that people can get hurt. Sometimes they die.

I've taught my son these values and I'm proud to say he's a chip off the old block.

Despite our move to the Upper West Side, my sister and I remained at our old grammar school in Harlem. It was nice to have that normalcy in our lives. The Upper West Side wasn't like Harlem. It was diverse, but there were definitely fewer people who looked like me. The farther south you went, the whiter it got. We now lived in a predominately white neighborhood. We went from being the majority to the minority. We were the only Black family in the entire apartment building. I wasn't bothered by it though. As a kid I was more worried about making friends than what my friends might look like.

Other than being in a new location, not much had changed for me, or so I thought. I had my school, my friends—old and new—I had my family, and I was happy. I was a kid. I wasn't thinking about how me being black and being in a white part of the city was the biggest change in our move.

As I adjusted to living in a new home in a new part of the city, I had to adjust to other things as well.

Black Behind the Shield

Something happened to me that I hadn't experienced before. I walked into a convenience store for a snack—some candy, or maybe a bag of chips. As I browsed the snack options, a security guard followed me throughout the store. It seemed odd. I thought he just happened to be walking around, but every aisle I turned down, there he was, staring at me. I left and shrugged it off to an untimely coincidence, but it continued to happen again and again at different stores.

It began to bother me, so one day I came home and asked my mother, "Why do I keep getting followed every time I go into a store?"

Her eyes softened and her smile faded as her disappointment grew, not with me but with the situation. While she'd anticipated this conversation, she'd hoped the day wouldn't come.

Her answer was simple. I was Black. She explained that unfortunately some people think kids who look like me are doing, or are going to do, something wrong. She told me not to be mad at them but to feel sorry that they chose to live like that. Then she expressed something that made me take a step back. My mother told me to never run to try to make it home on time. If I knew I was going to be late, I was to call to let her know, but I was never to run.

I stood there puzzled as hell. Did she just tell me that it's okay to be late? I didn't really want her to elaborate. It seemed like I'd just been given carte blanche to come home whenever I wanted. It also seemed like it could be a setup, but it turned out neither was the case. She explained that if a young Black boy is seen running down a city street, in my case Broadway, people would automatically assume that Black boy had gotten into trouble.

    This didn't make sense to me. I couldn't see why someone would automatically think I'd done something wrong. My mom went on to explain that if something had happened at that exact time I was running, they'd blame me. Because of what I looked like.

    I was only 13 but I was starting to recognize that being Black was a confinement, rather than merely a skin tone. Because I was Black, I didn't have the privilege of doing the same things my white friends could do. They were allowed to run down the street without worrying that it could be seen as a threat.

    I was hurt and disappointed. Even at that age I was witnessing first-hand the injustice rooted in our society. I told myself I'd never want another person, regardless of color, to feel the way I was feeling. Like anyone else, I should be able to feel comfortable walking into a store and browsing the aisles without arousing suspicion. As a kid, I hoped it would get better when I was older. Unfortunately, I am met with the same fate even today.

Chapter 4
THE TWINS

Growing up, I was fortunate to have friends from all different backgrounds. I had Black friends, Hispanic, white, Indian, and even Japanese friends. I grew up knowing that there are so many people who don't look like me but have much to offer. My friends liked me because of who I was and not what I looked like, just as I liked them.

My mother was, and still is, the main figure in my life who helped me develop into a caring human being. She taught me that the beliefs of most young people were directly related to their upbringing. Some parents, however, might have the best of intentions, but still do things that would be considered racist.

I had two white friends in my grammar school who happened to be twins. They were two of my best friends. We did everything together. We'd go to the park and play tackle football without equipment, go sledding on cardboard and even throw wet tissue paper out of their bedroom window and watch it sail in the air before landing on some unsuspecting neighbor's window. Don't ask me why. We did it all though. Our families were friends and it made for the perfect situation. They treated me like I was part of their family.

The twins' parents were successful lawyers. I didn't know what kind of lawyers they were. When you're young, a lawyer is a lawyer. I didn't know much about the law other than what I saw on TV, but when I heard the word "lawyer" I associated it with the police. Every time someone got arrested, the first thing they'd say, as they do today, is "I want a lawyer."

Being that I had aspirations of becoming a police officer one day, and because I was nosey, I asked their dad how it was to be a lawyer. I was given the boilerplate answer of it's a good job etc.... Maybe he thought I was too young to understand or maybe he didn't feel like talking about it.

What I really wanted to know was how many people that looked like me did he see when he was in court. I never had the courage to ask him that question, probably because I didn't want either one of us to feel awkward, but I bet it was a lot. It was always on my mind: were Black people treated the same in court as their white counterparts? I'd have to wait until I got older to get that answer. Oh, and the answer is a big fat NO!

The twins often invited me to sleep over at their house. It was usually a Friday night to Saturday. Back then cartoons only aired on the weekends. We looked forward to watching our main man Bugs Bunny, or Daffy Duck, or even the Flintstones. Ahhh, that's when TV was real. When Saturday morning rolled around, we'd park ourselves on the floor at the foot of their parents' bed. It was the most comfortable and it was the closet spot to the TV. We didn't care about our eyesight back then.

One time when I was on an overnight there, I happened to be sitting in my usual spot on the floor with my back up against the bed when I felt something strange.

My Afro, which was quite large back then, started moving. I felt fingers in my hair, and they weren't mine. It weirded me out. I didn't move because I figured out whose fingers they were: they belonged to the twin's father.

What the hell is this man doing with his fingers in my hair? But I just sat there. Unlike kids today, we respected our elders and never questioned them. This went on for about 10-15 seconds until he uttered, "Your people's hair just fascinates me."

Back then, being young and naïve, I hadn't grasped the realization of how racist a statement that was, but I did know it didn't sound right. I couldn't say anything though. I didn't know what to say. He was a great person and was like a father to me, so I didn't take his statement as I would today.

It did make me wonder how many Black people they knew. Did his amazement with my hair mask his real feelings, or was it simply curiosity? Was I the only one they knew that they could do this to?

Let's be clear, they were one of the most loving families I knew, but after being followed by security guards and now this, it highlighted the fact that I was different. I could only imagine how the police, in particular the white police, would treat me going forward. Though the only encounter I physically had with a white officer had been pleasant, I knew that for me things were going to get worse before they got better.

Chapter 5
MY FIRST TIME

    My grammar school years were fun, and I met a lot of friends. Other than the occasional "follow the leader" in a random convenience store it was one of the best periods of my life. My high school years, however, left something to be desired. I didn't like them much and I'm glad they're behind me. I went to an all-boy Jesuit high school in lower Manhattan. The only thing Black about my high school at that time was the hockey puck they called a hamburger that they used to serve us at lunch.
    When I say it was "mostly white," trust me, that's an understatement; but there were enough kids of color to make someone like me feel somewhat comfortable. The lack of color didn't stop me from making a lot of friends. I think it was easier for me to meet friends at first because I was on the football team.
    Playing football for me was my outlet. It was one of the few things in my life that gave me purpose and let me be me. I felt when I was on the field, or even in the locker room, people respected me because I was talented. There were a few of my white teammates who would tell racist jokes and mock some of the Black players for the way they walked. I ignored them and focused on football. When you're part of a team, in this case a football team, you might not always agree with or even like the guy

you're playing next to, but you put those differences aside for a common goal, which in football was winning.

When I became a state trooper it was like being on a football team in the sense that I occasionally worked with someone I didn't like or didn't get along with, but when we were out on the streets, we put those differences aside so we could make sure we'd both come home safely.

Being part of a football team helped me further understand people and taught me self-control, unless I was trying to take a player's head off on the field. I played cornerback, which allowed me to be aggressive and physical. It gave me the opportunity to let out all my frustrations.

One day our team was on the school bus heading to practice. Playing football in the city we didn't have the luxury of having our own football field at the school, so we had to take the school bus to this field in lower Manhattan full of dirt, rocks, and glass. I got more bruises from the practice field than I did the actual practice.

As we traveled to our practice field some of my white teammates noticed this brotha walking down the street wearing a sheepskin coat, which normally wouldn't have been a big deal, but it was over 80 degrees out. They thought it would be funny to yell out the windows of the school bus and make fun of him. One of them asked him if they wore those types of coats in Africa.

Annoyed with their racist remarks and obvious lack of common sense, I quickly moved to the other side of the bus because anyone with any sense knows you don't mess with someone wearing a sheepskin coat in 80 plus degree weather, which suggests that person may not be all there. At this point anything could pop off.

As luck would have it the bus slowed almost to a stop because of traffic. That's when that same brotha took this large-ass machete from inside his coat and darted towards the school bus windows. I never in my life heard so many "tough" guys screaming like little be-atches. Just as he approached the bus's windows the bus started to move again, lucky for their asses.

As soon as there was enough distance between the machete guy and us, I looked over at these shaking little loudmouths and with a big smile on my face said, "I bet you dumb asses won't do that again."

I didn't elaborate on the foolishness of their actions, but it was satisfying to see those guys cower like a bunch of punks.

I learned a lot about being on a team and what people will do or say when they think they can't be touched or harmed.

**

At my high school, most of the teachers were priests, and yes, it was as bad as it sounds. But I made the best of it, like always.

Some wondered why my Black ass would be at such a school in the first place, especially since I wasn't Catholic. The answer was simple: safety. Back in the day, a catholic school provided a quality level of instruction and discipline that you couldn't always find in a public school. The public schools were simply off the hook. I had friends at various public schools who told me they'd witnessed teachers getting beat up by students and desks thrown out of windows. That environment wasn't conducive to learning and I wanted no part of that.

Though the catholic school environment was good, the streets around my school weren't especially welcoming for a boy of color. When I walked around those streets, I'd notice that again I was being followed, but this time it wasn't by security guards at a store, it was by the actual police in their patrol cars. I'd occasionally see them out of the corner of my eye, driving like Miss Daisy's chauffeur. Just waiting for me to mess up so they could approach me. I was smart enough not to give them a reason. I ignored them and went about my business.

My school was all boys, meaning that there were no girls, duh. So, we had to rely on girls from neighboring all-girl schools to be our cheerleaders for football games or our guests at school dances.

Speaking of school dances, there'd been information circulating in school about an upcoming school dance. I had no desire to go but a couple of my good friends told me they were going to check it out and wanted me to go with them. I really didn't want to, but after a little convincing I was like, "What the heck, it couldn't be that bad."

When the night of the dance arrived, my goal was to go, have fun, dance with a few of the girls, and then head home. That's exactly what I did. At least, I tried to.

I arrived at the dance along with my two friends and their girlfriends. Yep, there's nothing like being a fifth wheel.

The dance itself was okay. The typical girl stands by a wall until a boy makes a fool of himself, but I was determined to get my groove on. I was trying to get my Michael Jackson going when an argument broke out between a bunch of white kids and some Black and Hispanic kids. I was trying to ignore them, but some of these white kids started throwing the "N" word around like it was water. I was quickly regretting my decision to go to this stupid-ass dance.

    I found my friends and we decided to leave. The dance wasn't all that anyway, and with this soon-to-be fight about to happen there was no sense in staying.

    We headed out and walked to the corner store before going home. My two friends wanted ice cream, so they went inside while I waited outside with their girlfriends. How I ended up babysitting them while my friends got ice cream I'll never know.

    As I waited, the girls and I talked about the dance and other miscellaneous crap.

    The store happened to be next to the subway's exit/entrance. As we stood there talking, I could hear a train pulling into the station. Moments later people started to ascend the stairs from the subway. We didn't think anything of it because that was normal in the city. However, it was who came up the stairs that ended up being the problem.

    Five white girls with big-ass hair and tons of makeup walked to the top step and in a matter of seconds started spouting comments to the two girls I was standing with.

    I was already pissed because of my decision to go to the dance and having to deal with the racist crap that was brewing, so I was in no mood to deal with these five little wanna-be tough girls. They continued saying shit, so I politely told those girls, "Shut the hell up!"

One of the girls looked me straight in my eye and without hesitation said, "Fuck you nigger, I wasn't talking to you!"

That was the first time a white person, male or female, called me that to my face. For a second, I was like a deer in headlights. When I came to, I wanted to smack that clown makeup right off her face. Before I could utter any type of comeback, I looked past her where the boyfriends of the five girls had just ascended to the top of the train station steps. I said to myself, "You've got to be kidding me."

Where were my friends, you ask? That's a good goddamn question.

As I stood there, the boyfriend of the loudmouth girl asked me what the problem was. There were five of them and one of me, so I calmly told him there wasn't a problem, I just didn't appreciate the girls disrespecting my friends and that they should take a walk.

That didn't go over well.

He stuck out his chest and his voice got deep. "You don't fucking talk to my girl."

This was going to go bad.

There was something my father told me when I was younger that came to me without even thinking about it, and that was: if someone thinks you can fight, they'll test you, but if they think you're crazy, they'll leave you alone.

I took one big deep breath and stood motionless for a few seconds. My hands started to shake, and a tear rolled down my cheek. The inside of my body started to rumble like an erupting volcano.

I calmly walked over to this white VW bug that was parked directly in front of the store and I punched the hood of that car with all my might, leaving a softball-sized dent in the hood. (My bad to whoever owned that car.)

I turned slowly back to the group of guys and with the calmest and most controlled voice I had I said, "Who's first?"

The cockiness in their faces was replaced with fear. The girl's boyfriend was quick to tell me there was no problem, he just wanted to know what was going on.

"Who's first?" I repeated.

His chest deflated. He looked toward his boys who each grabbed their girlfriend, turned, and began to walk away. Apparently, they thought I was crazy enough to eat their hearts. Thanks, Pop, it worked!

As soon as the group walked out of sight, my friends came out of the store. I should've slapped both of them for leaving me to take care of those dudes by myself, but it was cool.

The girls explained what happened and my friends were grateful that I stood tall for their girls. They offered to buy me a burger, which I wasn't going to say no to.

I'm not gonna lie, it could've ended up a whole different way. I was doing the right thing for protecting some folks who couldn't protect themselves. However, being called a nigger by a white person for the first time sent chills down my spine. It still does. It was inevitable, and it needed to happen. It prepared me for the next time.

Black Behind the Shield

And for a Black man or woman there's always a next time. It never gets easier to hear, but it does highlight the ignorance of the person saying it, and in my eyes, it makes *them* look like the idiot, not me.

All the experiences I went through in high school, good and bad, helped better prepare me for the next step of my growth, which was college.

Chapter 6
COLLEGE

It was time to put on my big boy pants, leave the city that never sleeps, and trek north to the country, where I was about to begin a new chapter in my life: college. It was one of the most important parts of my soon-to-be adulthood. I tried to take my football talents to college, but after one full summer of college football camp and a few too many hits to the head yours truly had to call it quits.

There were a lot of differences between living in the city and living in the country. In the country, people felt a lot more comfortable coming up to you and starting a conversation. In New York City the only conversations you had with people you didn't know were, "Can you spare some change?"

In the city if you were hungry and had a craving for a slice of pizza at 2 a.m. all you had to do was walk down to the closest pizza joint to satisfy that appetite. In the country you're assed out.

In the city if you wanted to go dancing you waited until about 11 p.m. to head to the club. In the country: "What the hell is a club?"

I attended the University of Connecticut (UConn) in Storrs. When I went to visit the school, its beauty awed me. Picturesque, serene, and it didn't hurt that the ratio of girls to guys was 3:1. You take a young man from an all-boy high school in New York City and put him in an environment such as this and the decision to attend was an easy one.

It did take some adjusting though.

Growing up in the city and settling down in the country was a culture shock to my system. Especially when I looked out my dorm window and saw freakin' cows grazing in the pasture. That was the first time I'd seen an actual live cow in person. After seeing that, my Black ass was ready to go home. Most freshmen go through a homesick phase. Mine was enhanced by those damn cows.

Like my grammar and high schools, the campus was predominately white. I had practice being in that situation, so I should've been a pro.

College is probably the most important time in a person's life from a growth standpoint. It was for me. In college, people learn not only about themselves but also about other people. You learn about what a person is feeling by the way they're standing, their mannerisms, how they say certain things, and what they mean by them. I was prepared for that, being a "nosey" kid and all. Of course, there's that thing called an education, but knowing about yourself and other people can be just as important. Sometimes the "why" and "how" are just as important as the "what." If I'd spent a little more time on the "what," maybe I wouldn't have had to be there on the five-year plan.

I learned how to survive on my own and be responsible for my actions without Mom there to pick me up. I wasn't the best student, but I had a master's degree in street smarts, and I could read someone before they opened their mouth.

I also learned that quite a few people at my college lived sheltered lives. It was amazing to hear students say things like, "I bet most Black people have been arrested," or, "Did you have both parents growing up?"

I would've thought by college they'd have figured that out, but they're probably the same people who "have a Black friend."

College prepared me for life, and an eventual career with the state police. If I wanted to be the kind of law enforcement officer I'd envisioned—which was someone who could read people, understand them, empathize with them, and, most of all, respect them—then I had to pay attention to them. It was important not to be around just the Black community, but the white community as well.

When you're around people who don't look like you, have different backgrounds than you, and most of all are raised differently than you, you have the unique opportunity to learn the other side of the fence. If more white police officers today took the time to understand people in the Black communities, then maybe some of the racial injustice and senseless killings could stop.

My learning from other people didn't take long. I'd been at college for only a few hours when I got my first taste of what campus life was going to be like.

My mom and I had just arrived on campus with all my crap in tow. We had trouble finding my dorm because the campus was so big, but eventually we found my living quarters. It was an old rustic dorm on the outskirts of campus. The doors to the rooms were made of very thin wood, the kind not suitable for late night dormitory life. Not that I would know anything about that.

As my mom and I were moving my belongings into my room, the sound of footsteps coming down the hall was accompanied by this loud, whiney voice. With every step the voice got louder until the footsteps stopped and that loud whiney voice was in my doorway.

There stood this skinny white kid. We both looked at each other for a few seconds. I introduced myself. He responded in kind and told me he was my roommate. I was like, "Hell naw." This kid couldn't be my new roommate. Right off the rip I could tell he was one of those guys who had to be the center of attention. It was going to be a long a semester if I had to live with him and that whiney voice, but that was the hand I was dealt, so I was all in.

His father entered our room and introduced himself to my mom and me. He appeared mild-mannered and pleasant.

My mom and I continued to move my stuff into my new "home." My roommate was in the hallway talking to his father, and out of nowhere he said, "What the fuck Dad, I thought I told you...!"

I looked at my mom. We stood there frozen, shocked.

Where I was from if I even thought of saying something close to what just came out of my roommate's mouth, I would've been knocked into next year, so that's what I was waiting for.

The opposite happened. His father apologized.

This was some Twilight Zone crap. I knew at that moment he and I were going to have a problem. If his father would take that from him, did he think I would? Not in this lifetime my man!

There was an aura about him that gave off a sense of entitlement. In my head, the only thing he'd be entitled to from me would be an ass whuppin.

We finished moving me in and it was time for my mother to head back home. It was tough saying goodbye, but it was my time now. Before she left, we made a quick trip to the bookstore so we could stock up on T-shirts and other UConn paraphernalia.

When we got there, it didn't take long for us to notice what UConn had in store for me. We both saw a T-shirt on a mannequin located at the front of the store that had the words "Huskies, Huskies, Huskies" printed on the front in a diagonal fashion. Probably not a big deal to most, but the "K" from each word was considerably bigger than the other letters and in a different color, which made it stand out from across the store: "KKK."

I'd like to believe it was unintentional, but as they say, "The eyes don't lie," and in this case neither did the T-shirt.

We headed back to her car trying to un-see what we just saw. As she was about to depart, she had one last piece of advice for me, and it had nothing to do with my behavior on campus, or what we saw in the bookstore. It had to do with my new roommate. She wanted to make sure I didn't judge him based on first impressions. She was diplomatic and chalked it off to him having a bad day and that he probably wasn't a bad guy, just a little different.

I didn't really believe that, but I stored the information, nonetheless.

That incident with my roommate did open my eyes to the fact that I'd meet other people in college who had similar personalities. I'd have to find a way to deal with them or it would be a long four years (five years, in my case).

That was an important thing that my roommate indirectly taught me. His quirkiness, cockiness and that aforementioned sense of entitlement would, at some point, have to be dealt with. He'd learn that those traits did not give him the right to use them with me.

After a small in-room incident when he accused me of something I didn't do he quickly realized he wasn't in Kansas anymore. I checked him on the spot. We ended up sitting down and clearing the air, and eventually we became good friends.

His behaviors had to be learned from someone or somewhere while he was growing up, and even though he took responsibility for his actions, there had to be a reason for them.

When my roommate's dad would come up to visit him, my roommate was like a different person. He was nice and not disrespectful. I'd like to think I had a part in that, but I guess we'll never know.

His dad coming to visit him made me wonder why my dad never came to visit me. I'd occasionally ask him to come up, but was always given a different excuse, which bothered me. I assumed he would when he could. I really couldn't worry about that though. I had school to focus on, which was enough to deal with.

Chapter 7
UNDER HIS WING

It was early in my first semester at UConn, and I was doing what I did best—minding my business as I navigated my way through campus. I felt like a tourist. I was seeing things here at school, and in the country, I'd never seen before. I was looking at everything.

One day a cop car approached me. I didn't think much about it because I was minding my own business. The car got closer, got right up on me. I thought to myself, *Didn't I leave all this cop-following-me nonsense in New York?*

The car pulled up next to me and I got a glimpse of the cop driving this ugly-ass cop car. He was Black which surprised me.

I was more surprised when the car stopped, and he motioned for me to come over. Had he mistaken me for someone who might've done something stupid earlier, and I just happened to "fit the description,"? That would've been par for the course.

I was hesitant at first. A cop was a cop, and if I didn't do anything wrong then he had no reason to be talking to me. But I figured what the hell. There wasn't much he was going to do to me with all these students around, especially since I was minding my own business.

I strolled over and said, "What's up?"

He was a short man and when he responded he had this raspy voice, but his smile would light up a room. I ain't gonna lie, he got me to let my guard down because of his charisma. I could read people, and there was something about him I trusted.

He seemed to understand I was hesitant. He told me I didn't have to worry and that I wasn't in any trouble. He just wanted to introduce himself to me.

My radar went up. Cops don't come up and say hi, especially to some college kid.

"That's cool," I said, "but why?"

He told me he took it upon himself to get to know as many Black students on campus as he could. He explained that he was the only Black cop in the UConn Police Department, and he felt that we (Black students and him) should stick together.

"We have to look out for one another," he said.

I thought his department must not like him or something if he had to make friends with the students, but I could see the sincerity in his eyes and in the way he carried himself. He meant what he said, and I had to appreciate that.

I told him I wanted to become a police officer and it was like his own kid had just done something that made him proud. He suggested I follow my dreams.

"Communities need more, good young Black police officers," he said. "There aren't enough."

He gave me his card, which I still have, and told me that if I ever needed anything to hit him up. I felt he was taking me under his wing, like his little protégé. We shook hands and as quickly as he appeared he disappeared.

I continued doing what I was doing best, which was minding my own damn business.

He was the kind of police officer I wanted to be. No agenda or hidden motives, he wanted to be nice, and to help. In my eyes most cops weren't like that. Now I was as determined to try to change the narrative as I'd been when I was a kid.

Later I'd try to sponge as much information as I could from him—anything I thought would help me on the road to becoming an upstanding member of a police department. Like my mom always says, everything happens for a reason. I was beginning to understand the reason he and I met that day.

As the days and weeks of my college life flew by, I'd see him on occasion. He'd wave as he drove by with that same big smile. Sometimes we'd stop and chat it up for a few. Sometimes making me miss class. Okay, so I used him as an excuse to miss class, don't judge me.

I was walking through campus one day and I saw him, but with no smile. Something was up. I did my best trying to wave him down without looking like a crazy person.

He stopped, but damn near drove over me. I guess I'd pretty much jumped in front of his car.

I walked up to his driver's window. He looked straight-up pissed. Part of me was afraid to say anything, but I'd developed a friendship with him so I felt I could. I point-blank asked him, "What the hell happened?"

"I'm good," he said softly.

"Cut the shit brah and tell me what's bothering you."

He wasn't going to tell me, and I didn't press any further.

He looked at me with anger in his eyes. "As a Black man you, unfortunately, are held to a higher standard than the white man."

I was caught off guard. This was not the guy I knew. Why would he tell me that? I didn't ask, I just nodded. "Okay."

"Watch yourself," he said. As he drove off.

By the tone of our conversation, I guessed something racial must've happened at work. He had refrained from going into details. I believe he didn't want to discourage me from my dreams of becoming a police officer. I respected that, but wished he'd told me. He never did.

He unwittingly reinforced what I already knew, what I'd experienced. People will treat me differently because of the color of my skin, even if I was a cop.

One thing I noticed about being a Black man at a predominately white school was that all my white friends expected me to be comfortable in my surroundings because they were. They had no idea what it was like to be the odd man out every time you went somewhere. To them I was comfortable because that's the way I made it look. I learned from a young age that I could fit in anywhere because of the person I was, not because of what I looked like.

Being in the country made me miss the comforts of Harlem. At home I didn't have to answer silly questions like, "You're from Harlem? Do you carry a knife?" The best one was, "Have you ever shot anyone?"

The dumb questions kept rolling in. I answered most of them the same way: "Do you?" or "Have you?" They'd follow it up with the preverbal, "I didn't mean anything by it."

My life in college continued. Everything was different but remained the same. I did what a number of college students did on the weekends: I headed home to see family. I'd always spend the beginning of my weekend at home telling my mom how college was going of course leaving out the juicy details. I didn't see Pop very much, I guess because all my friends were living near my mom. I'd see him on occasion, but that took a turn when I went to see him on one of my trips home.

He and I had been hanging out and shooting the shit at his apartment. I was filling him in on how school was going and about all the beautiful girls that were on campus. He was hearing me but wasn't listening to me. Our conversation continued when out of the blue he asked me for money. *Why is my dad, the principal, asking me for money?*

He told me he was short, but he'd pay me back. I thought it was odd, but I ignored my gut and gave it to him.

When it happened again on another visit, I knew he was into something he shouldn't be. I didn't want to ask him about it, so I gave him the money. But that was the last time I ever did.

The fact that he only asked for a small amount of money made me more curious. If it had been a lot at least I could rationalize the fact that he needed it to get through the week. Maybe this was why he never came to visit me at school.

When you love someone, you want what's best for him or her, and it's difficult to say no. After that, when I'd come home on a weekend, I'd see my mom and my friends, but not Pop. I didn't want to be put in that situation anymore. Part of me figured if I let time pass, everything would work itself out.

When I'd return to college from being home, I'd think about him often, but I had to control my life.

I was having fun at school, but the Black men and women on campus were still being treated differently. Most of the time it wasn't blatant, but I'm not sure that was better.

I needed to not just talk about it but also to be about it, to figure a way to educate some of my white sheltered friends so they could understand what I, and the rest of the Black community, was all about. I hoped whatever I shared with them would be taken to heart and perhaps rub off on their friends.

Chapter 8
SCHOOL IS IN SESSION

Teaching is more than 123s and ABCs. Teaching is that ability—or knack, if you will—to enlighten, to help someone learn something they didn't already know. You can tell someone how to tie his or her shoes or ride a bike, but most can't learn it until you show them. What you can't teach someone is what it's like to be Black. No matter what you do they will never completely understand, but what you *can* do is show them. Give them a little taste of what it is you go through and have to deal with on a daily basis.

There was this brotha who lived in my dorm and he and I were the only two. He was a good dude. He and I understood each other. He'd always try to get me to go to happy hour. He knew I didn't drink but that didn't stop him from trying. He finally twisted my arm one day and I went.

It didn't end up well for me.

He and I would always end up in some deep conversation that ended with me saying, "Dude, I don't get it." But one thing we often discussed that we both understood was that our white friends in our dorm seemed to be clueless when it came to anything that had to do with Black people. Some would tell us they had no Black kids in their high school, and if they did, they could count them on two fingers. Some would say that they had a Black friend growing up, but that statement alone made us want to slap some reality into them. They didn't know anything about how we were raised, what it was like to be different than everyone else. Hell, they didn't even know what a good ass whuppin felt like. Our plan was to change that. Change their perception, not the ass whuppin.

My friend loved New York and would occasionally go with me when I'd go home to visit my family. There we came up with an idea: on our next trip we'd bring a couple of our white friends from our dorm and give them a little "taste" on how the other half lived. If we did this there was going to be a discussion afterwards simply because it was something they'd never experienced. At least, that's what we were hoping. The more we talked about it the more we wanted to do it. In our own twisted way, it was like some sort of payback. A cultural ass whuppin if you will.

We picked our two most sheltered white friends. One was a girl who truly didn't know one thing about a Black person, the other was a guy who acted like he knew but he didn't. When we approached them about taking a day trip to New York City I had to make it sound like we were going to Rockefeller Center or somewhere touristy like Central Park. If we'd told them, we were taking them to Harlem they would've glued their asses to their dorm rooms and wouldn't have come out until we were gone.

The day came and we were set to leave. I had a car on campus but decided that we'd take the bus. I knew where the bus would drop us off and it'd be less of a headache than trying to find parking everywhere.

Black Behind the Shield

Our two friends were excited, but their dumb asses had no idea what was in store for them. We got to the bus, and they kept asking, "What are we going to do first?" I told them sightseeing because that's what we were going to do. They just didn't know where.

The bus ride was long, but we finally arrived in New York City. We transferred to a city bus that would take us directly into the heart of Harlem.

As the bus traveled through Harlem our friend's noses were pressed against the window like dogs in a car. They saw masses of people, which I knew they weren't used to, and among those masses of people none of them were white, which they definitely took notice of. The sounds of car horns blaring and people yelling were also a culture shock for them.

As the bus neared our stop the girl noticed a rope suspended between a pair of 3-story brownstone buildings and on that rope were clothes held on by wooden clothespins. She asked me why they had clothes hanging on a rope. *My god!* I would've figured she'd have seen a clothesline in a cartoon at least. I told her not everyone was as fortunate as her to have their own washer and dryer. That they had to hand wash their clothes and then hang them out to dry. She was amazed, but the guy we'd brought looked at her like she was stupid. I looked at him with this wry smile as if to say, "Don't worry, you'll get yours."

As they continued to peer out the window at the wonders of Harlem, the bus arrived at our stop with the bus driver calling out, "125th Street."

My friend and I looked at our two unsuspecting white friends and told them it was our stop. They both looked at us like we'd been smoking something. They didn't want to be rude, but they didn't want to get off the bus either. You could sense their hesitation from a mile away. We were trying not to laugh. The only people paying attention to them were us.

We led them off the bus and there we stood, right in the middle of Harlem on 125th street. The iconic Apollo Theater was just down the street. They were truly the only white people as far as the eye could see, and they were uncomfortable.

We began to walk the streets of Harlem. Neither of them said anything. We didn't say much to them, we didn't want to take away from their moment in the spotlight. The white girl was so scared she had a vice grip on the other guy's arm and didn't realize it.

My friend and I slowed down until they passed in front of us, then we stopped and let them continue walking. They kept on, having no idea we'd stopped. We were going to hide but thought better of it just in case.

When they realized we weren't with them, the look on their faces was priceless.

They walked back to us and asked us why we stopped. We told them we wanted them to take in all the city has to offer by themselves.

We walked for a good while before we decided to end their experience and jump in a cab towards Times Square.

During our ride to Times Square, we asked them what they thought about Harlem. They both said they were a little nervous because they were the only white people there. I asked them if anyone gave them dirty looks or said anything to them that was inappropriate.

"No," they both responded.

"Then why would you be nervous?"

They had no answer.

"I guess I should be nervous at UConn being that I'm often always the only Black guy in a class or in a room, then, right?"

Again, neither had anything to say.

My friend and I let them know that being Black in a white school is something we had to deal with daily, yet we were supposed to be good with that. Meanwhile, they were the only white people in a Black part of town for barely thirty minutes and they couldn't take it. At school they expected Black people to be comfortable around them but they're the ones who have a problem being comfortable around us. It was what you might call a Confucius moment. They both realized that we were right and understood where we were coming from.

Years later, a very dear and great friend of mine, who is white and who I went to college with and golf with on occasion, explained that they reacted like that because they were conditioned to see Black people that way. He told me that if he was walking down a street and saw three Black guys coming toward him, he'd feel more intimidated than he would if those same three guys were white. It wasn't because he was racist, it was just the way he and most white people have been conditioned. And he's right.

The two friends that we took on this little excursion explained that their feelings toward Black people wasn't racial, it was more fear of the unknown and their ignorance. These two were good people and good friends. They thanked us for the experience.

The rest of the trip we spent laughing about our time in Harlem, and when we got back to school, I could tell there was something different about both of them, but in a good way. Our hope was that they'd be more comfortable around people of color, and, after that field trip, we thought they were.

Chapter 9
IT'S ALL CLEAR NOW

I went to college with the intention of graduating and getting a job in my field of study, whatever that would be. I figured I'd leave it up to what interested me the most, in case being a police officer didn't work out.

I started off as a psychology major, then switched after one semester to Human Development and Family Relations. Sounds important but it really wasn't. I switched because there were more girls in that major. Just keeping it real. Honestly, I didn't know what I was going to do with either major. But what I did know was that I wanted to be a police officer. My only question was what branch? Was I going local, state, or federal? I had no idea until one fall evening.

I'd gotten a job as a bouncer/doorman at a bar on campus known as "Huskies." I wasn't too keen on working at a bar. The only reason I did it was because there were always long lines to get in and yours truly was not waiting in any lines. So, if I worked there, poof, there go the lines.

Being a bouncer had its pros and cons. Along with no waiting in any lines, I could eat for free, which was huge for any college student. However, the downside was you had to clean up at the end of the night after all these drunk-ass kids and you also had to deal with any arguments or altercations between these same drunk-ass kids. There was always something going on. In some ways I felt like a babysitter or even a mini cop, but without a badge or gun or any damn sense. This job, however, would end up being a blessing in disguise.

During one fall evening I was working the door at Huskies on one of the busiest nights of the week. With busy comes people, alcohol, and problems. The crowds that night looked like any other night. Girls were wearing next to nothing trying to be cute and the guys were wasting all their money trying to impress them.

The night continued without a hitch until I heard, "Matt, fight!"

I jumped off my stool like there was a fire and ran with the other bouncers to the rear of the bar. When we got there this dude was sitting on the floor with a gash in his head. I was no EMT, so I was gonna give him a Band-Aid and call it a day. The guy who apparently clocked him was still standing there so we grabbed him and kicked him out of the bar. Unbeknownst to me the police were called. When a guy's bleeding all over the floor, I guess it was a no-brainer.

Another bouncer and I waited outside for the police to arrive so we could point out the two guys who were involved in the fight. I thought campus police would be the ones coming but I learned that night there was this little thing called "jurisdiction." The bar happened to be just outside of campus property. That area was covered by the state police.

I'd heard of the Connecticut State Police but never saw one in person or knew anything about them. I was eager to see one so I could get an idea of what they were like.

In the distance, the night sky became bright with the flashing of blue and red lights. As each second went by the lights got brighter and brighter and before you knew it two police cruisers barreled into the parking lot, coming to a screeching halt.

When the crowd saw the police, they scattered. Some went back into the bar. Others stood frozen because the two cruisers had blocked off an avenue of retreat. Everyone stood and waited to see what was going to happen next. I did, too.

From these two cruisers exited two rather large state troopers. Both were wearing fly-ass gray uniforms with royal blue and yellow stripes going down a grayish black pair of pants, a royal blue tie against a grey shirt, a shiny gold badge pinned to their chest and topped off with a gray state police Stetson with royal blue tassels. Yo! I gotta tell you, they had the sharpest uniforms I'd ever seen on any police officer in my life.

Now that they had my attention, I wanted to see how they operated. They apparently didn't need my help figuring out who was involved in the fight and did so quickly. After a few brief conversations with the patrons and the two involved in the fight they arrested both of them. As quickly as they arrived, they vanished.

It was clear to me now. I knew what I wanted to be: a Connecticut State Trooper. There was no doubt or hesitation. I was not only impressed by their uniforms, which were mad sharp, but it was their professionalism and demeanor that sold me. They commanded respect once they exited their police cruisers, but they also gave respect when they were talking to the people in the parking lot. The only thing left for me to do was figure out how to become one.

I was enjoying college and working at Huskies but now I had found my calling.

I was having the time of my life until I got an unexpected phone call from my mom. I could tell by her voice that something wasn't right. It was the kind of feeling you get when you're trying to figure out if you should slowly peel your Band-Aid off or just say the hell with it and rip it off. I wanted her to rip it off and tell me what was up.

She eventually told me my dad had been arrested for buying drugs. Initially I was pretty calm. I believed that was an inevitable result of his ways, but then a range of emotions came over me all at once. Inside, I was pissed, embarrassed, and sympathetic, but most of all I was concerned. This was a high-profile case. He was a principal, and it was going to affect not only him but the rest of my family. I needed time to think, and figure shit out.

I went back to Huskies, thinking if I worked and was around friends my mind would be clear and that would help me figure out what to do. As fate would have it, I ended up being approached by a college buddy of mine. When he approached me, he had this smile on his face like he'd just heard a joke.

"Yo Matt, do you have a twin?"

I'm sure my confused look prompted him to continue. He told me he was reading the newspaper and a guy with the same name as me had been arrested for buying crack in New York City.

With a stoic face I responded, "That was my dad."

Thank God my mom broke the news to me first. I would've been devastated to hear it from someone outside the family.

His smile quickly disappeared, and he began to apologize repeatedly. I told him not to worry about it, but I had to get out of there before someone said the wrong thing.

It took me a few days to gather my thoughts, but when I did, I called my dad. He wouldn't answer the phone, so I kept calling until he did. When he finally answered he spent the first few minutes crying on the phone telling me how sorry he was. I told him he should be crying, and he should be sorry, but that was never going to stop me from having his back and loving him. I told him we'd get through it, but when his case was over, he had to get help. He said he would. I knew enough to know, with someone addicted to drugs, not to believe it until it happened.

That was how my senior year kicked off. By the time I graduated, I'd done all my homework and information gathering about the state police and applied.

The testing period was a grueling nine-month process. I had to take a written exam, a physical, a polygraph, a psychological written and oral exam, and a background check followed by a medical. After all that they were only taking 80 recruits out of approximately 5200 candidates who applied. My chances of success were slim.

I waited by the phone every day, prepared for whatever the results were going to be. When the call finally came, the lady on the other end of the line started talking and all I heard was blah, blah, blah until she said, "We would like to offer you a position with the state police. Do you accept?"

I couldn't say "Yes" quick enough. It was what I'd been waiting for since I was a kid. I was finally going to be part of the law enforcement community.

I hung up the phone knowing that the easy part was over. Now I had to prepare myself mentally and physically for a grueling seven-month make-or-break experience at the state police academy.

Part 2: THE SHIELD

Chapter 10
THE ACADEMY

I was told that the Connecticut State Police academy was one of the hardest in America. Inside I was like, *Please, how hard can it be? Seven months? I could do seven months on my back!*

I said as much to friends and felt pretty cocky about it. But inside I also knew, despite all that yappin', I was about to find out what I was really made of.

The Sunday night before I had to report to the academy, my stomach was in knots, and I had to crap at least twice before I went to bed. The minute I got up I'd have to start backing up all that talking I was spewing about how the academy couldn't be that bad. It couldn't be completely easy because you only got to come home on the weekends. Mondays to Fridays you belonged to them.

I got up early that Monday morning— "zero-dark-thirty" early. I was scrambling around trying to make sure I had everything. The last thing I wanted to do was show up without something and get singled out for it. My plan was to blend in for seven months. I wanted to be as anonymous as humanly possible.

I packed my car and made the thirty-minute trip to Meriden, Connecticut, home of the Connecticut State Police Academy.

Black Behind the Shield

I could see it. Just up the hill. A hill, by the way, I'd soon be running up and down for the next seven months, although I didn't know that as I drove into the academy.

Before I could stop my car, I had instructors yelling and screaming at me to do this and to go here. What the hell had I got myself into?

I jumped out of my car that was barely in park and ran with all my stuff to the dormitory. You saw other recruits doing the same thing. Some were dropping their typewriters (yes, typewriters, we didn't have computers, or cell phones, for that matter). I saw a few recruits faint.

One recruit stopped to help one of those who'd fainted and got yelled at and was made to do pushups. DAMN, I thought. I wasn't going to help anybody.

We all finally made it to our rooms and were told to stand at attention outside by our doorways. Remember how I wanted to stay anonymous and blend in? I looked around out of the corner of my eye. Of the 80 recruits, maybe 12 were Black. Instead of blending in, I was standing out.

It got worse. One of them left after the first night. Another dropped out soon after.

Unfortunately, many years later we lost one of the other ten to cancer. He'd volunteered to help at the World Trade Center immediately after the 9/11 attacks. Rest in peace good brotha!

Another part of my notion that this couldn't be that bad also disappeared quickly. It was one of the toughest things I'd ever been through. You go in knowing that they're going to play head games with you but somehow, they fill your body and head with so much stress you can't keep up with it no matter what you know inside.

Like the military, in the beginning they try to break you down—hard. They test your will and determination constantly and under higher and higher stress situations. If you're not ready for that type of mental beat down, then the Connecticut State Police isn't for you.

There was also the physical beatdown, which was part of the stress and just as constant. Those who were left standing and still had all their appendages moved on.

We did pushups on top of pushups. I did so many sit-ups you could bounce a quarter off my abs. We ran so much that walking felt like a reward. We got yelled at so often that when I was home on the weekends, I found myself sitting in silence listening to nature just to enjoy the peace and quiet. I've never been a nature guy.

To get through all of that I decided early on that, if they wanted me gone, they'd have to physically pick my ass up and throw me out. Quitting wasn't an option.

The Connecticut State Police is a paramilitary organization. Everything they do is regimented and has a purpose, right down to the simplest activity. For example, when we'd go to lunch in the dining hall, it was usually after a long run. We only had a certain amount of time to eat our food and be back in the dormitory showered and ready for the next block of instruction. If we weren't ready then it was back on the ground doing push-ups, sit-ups, and whatever ungodly exercises they could come up with. To this day, I'm not late for anything.

Black Behind the Shield

I remember one day being in our Accident-Investigation class, which had been conveniently scheduled right after lunch. The instructor was the epitome of what you'd think a trooper looked like. He was big, tall, square-chinned and had a deep voice—like a white Barry White—and wore his Stetson just above his eyes. He was thorough in his lectures and despite being intimidating and strict he was a good guy. The only problem was that, unlike Barry White, he was monotone in his delivery. Being in his class after exercising, eating, and showering, one would be ready for night-night. Oh, and they kept it warm in the classroom. All the ingredients for a lovely nap.

When the class first began, he told all the recruits that if we ever got tired to simply raise our hand and we'd be allowed to stand at the back of the classroom until we felt more awake. Ha-ha! Come on man. That was a trap. Yours truly wasn't falling for it. I was born at night, not last night.

But it's not as if I didn't want to. I was sitting with my hands on my desk, forcing my eyes to stay half open. It felt as if someone had tied bricks to my eyelids. As tired as I was, my hand was not going in the air to ask for relief.

As the class continued my body was at the brink of exhaustion. I looked out of the corner of my eye and saw one of my friends raising his hand. The instructor hadn't asked any questions, so I knew what he was about to do. In my head I was saying, "NOOOOOO," but my body and face said, "you're on your on dawg."

The instructor with his square chin and deep voice looked at my friend and said, "Yes?"

My friend, with a bit of nervousness in his voice, said, "Sir, I'm tired. May I stand at the back of the room, Sir"?

By this point I was wide awake. I wanted to see what was going to happen next.

The instructor, with an almost "I got ya," tone in his voice, said," Go ahead."

My friend stood and walked to the back of the classroom.

The instructor, while facing the chalkboard and not missing a beat, said to my friend, "Run in place. Begin."

All you could hear was the "tick, tick, tick" coming from his high-gloss military black shoes as each step hit the floor.

I looked at my friend's face and almost burst out laughing. This was the same guy who showed up at orientation that Friday before the academy was to begin in a red-and-white Adidas jump suit with white sneakers and thick red laces.

Everyone else was in a suit.

You would've thought he was a member of Run D.M.C. When one of the instructors asked him why he was dressed like that he replied at the top of his lungs, "Sir! I already have the job, Sir!"

I knew from that day on we were going to be friends.

As the class went on, a giant puddle of sweat formed under his feet and his shirt looked like he'd been in a sauna. There was so much sweat on the ground it sounded like he was running in the rain.

Black Behind the Shield

About five to ten minutes had passed when the instructor, with calm in his voice and not looking up, said to the recruit, "Recover," which was another way of saying, "Sit your dumb ass down and don't ask me no more stupid questions."

My friend took his seat out of breath and drenched with sweat. We caught eyes for a moment and both of us started cracking up, but we had to do so discreetly. The last thing I wanted was to relive that whole ordeal only with me. To this day every time we bring that incident up, we can't stop laughing.

As the academy got into full swing and the recruits got more comfortable with each other, several of the white recruits would talk to me like I didn't belong. I had one ask me if there was a quota of the number of Blacks that they needed to have. He tried to ask it innocently, but I could read between the lines. I responded by saying that it was probably the same quota that got his ass accepted.

We had a few racist recruits in my class. Unfortunately, those same recruits were going to graduate and take their racist mentality to the streets.

The days turned into weeks and the weeks turned into months. We learned everything from accident and motor-vehicle investigation to public speaking. We learned how to shoot a gun. There was an ethics class, but it was more about if you should take that free cup of coffee from the restaurant. That was a waste of time. When I graduated, I was sent every night, because I was a rookie, to go pick up a bag full of free donuts from the local donut shop. Yep, cops and their damn donuts!

One thing they didn't teach us, which in hindsight they should have, was what to do when your fellow trooper is doing something illegal or harmful to a member of the community. It was always preached that we have to stick up for each other, and the badge means everything, and yada yada yada but the fact remains that this was a key component that was missing then and seems is still missing from today's law enforcement curriculum.

There was and still is an unwritten rule that we take care of each other no matter what. I believed that, to a certain extent. We had to protect each other and keep each other safe. That was your brother or sister you were working with, and it was our job to make sure each one of us came home safe after every shift.

Yes, it was a dangerous job, and we had to protect each other, but to what extent?

Today that unwritten rule is being used by some police officers to take people's constitutional rights away or cause them injury or death just because that officer can, and that's a problem.

The academy can't teach you to have empathy, to be compassionate, to have understanding and to not be a racist. You either possess these traits and behaviors or you don't. It's like I used to tell my children when they were young. If a good and honest person hits the lottery for five million dollars, then they're a good and honest person with five million dollars to do more good things with. However, if a bad person comes into that same amount of money, then they're still bad but now they have more money to do more bad things with. The same thing goes for a police officer. If a kindhearted and compassionate person becomes a police officer, they, along with the power bestowed on them, have the ability to make situations less combative, and they can understand and empathize with different types of people in their community. This makes their job easier, and the lives of the people they're sworn to protect safer. However, if a racist becomes a police officer, then those same powers bestowed on him or her are more likely to be used to commit senseless acts of violence towards the people they have hatred for, without any fear of retaliation. They're the police.

As my time in the academy drew toward an end, I realized I had learned a lot of important lessons from some very knowledgeable instructors who I thought were the best at what they did. And for the most part my classmates were top notch. I wasn't going to let a couple sour apples spoil the friendships I'd made with all the other great recruits who were soon to be troopers.

Today is no different. There are so many great men and women who are tremendous police officers, but they're getting outshined by the ones who continue to commit horrendous and despicable acts of violence in our communities, in particular the Black community.

They do teach you that the job is stressful, and that you'll be put into life-changing situations, and yes, you might have only seconds to make a decision, but none of that gives any police officer the right to unleash havoc on someone because of the color of their skin.

The academy tested my patience when they yelled at me. They tested my determination when they made me do crazy amounts of exercises, my comprehension during the vigorous classes on police procedures, my ability to handle stress in the firearms training and defensive driving, but most importantly, the academy did their best to make me a well-rounded state trooper. I happened to be a well-rounded person who became a state trooper, not a state trooper who became a well-rounded person. The job never defined who I was, it became part of who I was. I'll forever be grateful to them for that.

    The academy could only prepare me for police procedures and how to enforce the law. They couldn't prepare me for the racism I'd unfortunately encounter while doing this great job.

Chapter 11
THE BROTHA PATROL

Upon graduation from the academy, I got assigned to Troop K in Colchester, Connecticut. To give you an idea of the kind of town the troop was in, its nickname from some was "Clan-chester," and if you couldn't tell by its nickname it was made up of mostly white people. That didn't make it a bad town, just a town where people like me would stick out.

Connecticut is made up of mostly white Americans, with the cities of Bridgeport, New Haven, and Hartford housing most of Connecticut's minorities. In the early 1990's, when I began my career, Connecticut was one of the homes of the Ku Klux Klan, also known as the KKK. One of the former leaders of a KKK chapter based in Connecticut made his home in Wallingford, Connecticut before he and some of his associates were arrested on various gun charges and a variety of hate crimes against minority groups. The highest-ranking leader, or the Imperial Wizard also resided in Connecticut. This isn't to say all the white people in the state were racists or Klan. They weren't. But, from my experience, it (the Klan) was significant at the time.

The troop I worked at covered about thirteen towns, with one trooper responsible for anywhere from two to four towns by his/herself a night. What was it like? Imagine one manager trying to cover two to four restaurants every night by themselves. That's exactly how it felt when I went to work.

As a rookie I worked the midnight shift. Most rookies did when they first got on the job. It wasn't bad, but sometimes it got a little slow. There were a few other troopers from my academy class who were also assigned to Troop K, only one of whom was Black. We were the only two troopers of color in the entire troop and we both worked midnights. He was mad cool and could make a hell of a cheesecake.

As new troopers, we all got assigned field-training officers (FTOs). All my FTOs were on point. They knew the procedures, but they also knew how to teach you without being overbearing, all the while keeping you safe. Unfortunately, there were a couple of FTOs who took the fact that they had more seniority than the rookies to demean and talk down to them. I guess that's part of being a rookie.

One of the new troopers was a female, and she ended up being my roommate when we graduated (strictly platonic). She'd come home and constantly bitch about her FTO and how he would treat her like garbage. I made a note of who he was and looked out for him, and one night he was assigned as my FTO, covering for my regular FTO on his night off.

I went into the night with an open mind. Just because she didn't get along with him didn't mean I wouldn't. If I went on patrol with him having predetermined notions of the kind of person he was, that would have shown, and being that I was on probation it would've looked bad for me. I was still trying to learn as much as I could.

We went out on patrol and stopped a few cars for speeding and other motor-vehicle violations. I continued to learn the area. When you're from a big city and you come to work in the country it's like jumping in a lake in the middle of the winter: nothing but shock to your system. Overall, the night was uneventful. We decided to head in early so we could do some paperwork. Unlike police on TV, we always had paperwork. A lot of paperwork.

When we got back to the troop his attitude changed a little, along with his gait. There was a cockiness to his walk, and his chest started to puff. I later found out that the other troopers secretly called him "Little Napoleon." This dude was only about five foot six and maybe 140 pounds but acted like he was 6'2" – 230. The guys used to steal his uniform shirts from the cleaning bin and have the sleeves taken in around the biceps, so he'd think his arms were getting bigger.

We were standing in the hallway amongst some other seasoned troopers when he said to me, "Yo! Go get me (some form) from the report room."

My mind said, "Who the hell do you think you're talking to?" But when I opened my mouth, "Sure," came out. There were other troopers there. I didn't want to embarrass him in front of them.

I got the form and returned. I called him over, away from the other troopers. He walked over with his puffed-out chest.

I said, "I'm not sure who you think you're talking to but I'm not your errand boy. If you need something, I'll be more than happy to get it for you." I handed him the form. "You'll ask me. You'll never tell me."

His chest visibly started to deflate. You could tell that no one had spoken to him like that, especially a rookie. He apologized and we never had a problem going forward.

Neither did my roommate. Probably because he knew that we lived together, and he didn't want any more problems.

After about six weeks all of us recruits were finally off the FTO program and took to the streets on our own. The other Black trooper and I stayed on the midnight shift with the hope of getting days when we had more seniority. As a result, we worked most nights together.

One particular night we were at roll call, and we could all hear the phones in the dispatch room ringing off the hook. There was this weirdness in the air that made my Spidey senses tingle.

After roll call the other Black trooper and I decided to go out on the highway and stop some cars for speeding or whatever else we saw. We were in the midst of giving a ticket to a very unhappy motorist when dispatch contacted me over the police radio. They wanted me to respond to a loud noise complaint. Without skipping a beat, I said "Roger" and headed to the complaint. The other trooper left with me and advised dispatch that he'd be backing me up. We pretty much did everything together while we were working and always had each other's back.

Black Behind the Shield

The complaint was in Colchester, so I didn't have to go far. We arrived at this small apartment building and could hear the music emanating from one apartment while we were standing outside. We entered the building and walked up to the second floor.

The music got louder and louder as we approached the apartment. After repeated knocks, one of the occupants opened the door.

There stood this young white girl, maybe in her mid 20's. She looked at me and the other trooper, laughed and shut the door in our face. We were in full uniform, topped off with our Stetsons that sat proudly on top of our heads. We looked at each other with the most bewildered look you could imagine.

"No, she did not just do that," I said, somewhat shocked.

"Uh, yep she did," my partner said.

I knocked on the door again, this time with a little more authority. The same girl opened the door. I immediately put my foot between the door and the frame so she couldn't close it. I stayed calm and asked her why she shut the door in my face.

"You guys ain't real" she said. "There's no Black cops in Colchester."

Her response fit the stereotype of "Clan-Chester."

"Yes, we are real." I grabbed my handcuffs. "These are real, too."

It took a minute to sink in. "Oh, my God," she said. "You're real freakin' troopers." She covered her mouth with her hand. "Sorry I shut the door on you like that. I never saw a Black trooper—let alone two—in this town before."

"Spread the word. We're here to stay."

We knew from that moment it was not going to be easy being a Black trooper at this barracks.

The night didn't end there. We got rerouted to a disturbance at one of the local bars. I was like, "We do have other towns to patrol, don't we?"

We arrived at this bar and, par for the environment, it wasn't very "color" friendly. As we walked in you could almost hear a pin drop. It was like that scene from 48 Hours with Eddie Murphy. I guess they hadn't seen us before either.

I asked the bartender what the problem was and as I was talking to her this Black woman started getting boisterous. My first thought was, *Damn sista, did you get lost?*

She kept saying to this older white gentleman, who looked like he was from the peace, love, and happiness era, to keep calling her what he had been. My partner and I exchanged looks. We both knew where this was headed.

I asked her, "What did he say?"

"He kept calling me nigger."

"Really?"

She confirmed it, along with the bartender.

The other trooper and I slowly walked over to where he was standing. My face was so close to his I could probably identify the type of beer he'd been drinking by his breath.

"Did you say to her what she's claiming?" I asked. "Because if you did that means you were referring to me and my partner as well. I don't think you'd do that, right?"

"No sir I wouldn't," he said nervously.

"Good! Then leave," I said.

He grabbed his belongings and exited with the quickness.

Unfortunately, it was within his rights to say what he wanted, but my goal was to de-escalate the situation. I thought telling him to leave was the best way. Back then that was the way we handled things. Since then, things have changed dramatically.

The woman was grateful and said she was happy to finally see some Black troopers in her town. We smiled and my partner and I left to go somewhere to chill for a bit. We never thought it would be like this, but now we knew it was, we needed to be ready for anything we could think of. Or so we believed.

Chapter 12
BIG BALLS

I always tried to be professional and maintain a sense of respect when dealing with the public, even if that same public didn't respect me because of the color of my skin. Working in mostly all-white towns tried my patience repeatedly, but I swore to serve and protect at all costs. Sometimes I'd give people more chances than they deserved, but that was the way I was. It would occasionally bite me in the ass, but somehow, I always ended up on top.

One summer night around 1 a.m., I got called to a loud-noise complaint. I was starting to think that all these country people did was make noise.

Dispatch sent me to this little spot called Lollipop Island, which was in the town of Lebanon. It was a small piece of land that extended into a lake and was shaped kind of like a lollipop, hence the name.

I drove my police cruiser to the entrance of this Lollipop Island. I didn't see anyone at first. I thought whoever was making the noise had bounced.

I turned off my cruiser and stepped outside to see if I could hear anyone. Surer than shit, voices were coming from near the water. For those of you who've never lived in or been in the country, the night can be very, very quiet. You can cough and be heard a half a mile away. If you're on or near the water, make it a mile.

Black Behind the Shield

I couldn't drive into this little stretch of land so instead I got back in my cruiser and shined my spotlight. Whoever was out there would know now that the police had arrived. Within a minute four kids, one girl and three guys, all white, appearing to be in their late teens, maybe early twenties, walked from the beach's entrance onto the road, looking to avoid the cop at the other end of that spotlight. But I'd seen them and approached on foot.

Right from jump street I could tell the guys were wannabe tough guys. The ringleader was a big kid who dwarfed me. I guess he felt like he was the man.

I've always believed that, as a cop, you talk first if you have the opportunity and act second. I kindly explained to them that I didn't mind if they stayed out all night, but they'd have to keep the noise down.

When you try to be nice, some people mistake that for weakness. Big mistake.

The ringleader took it to another level. In a loud, exaggerated voice he said, "What?!"

My buttons started to get pushed, but I held my ground and asked again if they would be quiet so that I didn't have to take it to *my* next level.

The girl they were with was obviously getting nervous and didn't want any part of any trouble. "Hey guys, let's go," she said.

I'm thinking, *Cool. Get the hell outta here so I can go about my business.*

They walked to the girl's car, got in, and she started to drive away.

My job was done. I got back in my cruiser and was about to take off when the girl's brake lights came on and the car stopped about 20 yards from where she started. I wasn't sure why she did that. Like at the circus, all three guys got out one after the other. This was trouble, and the girl must have known it. She drove away leaving me to deal with the three knuckleheads.

This was probably going to escalate so I called for my wingman to come back me up. He was about ten minutes away, so I had to hold down the fort until he got there.

The three guys started to walk down the road away from me, purposely being loud as they did. I pulled up in my cruiser about 10 feet away from them.

I told them that if they kept it up, they'd be arrested. The ringleader ignored me and started singing.

I kept up with them in my cruiser at a slow crawl while they kept making noise. Then my wingman arrived.

As soon as I saw his cruiser approaching, I drove up next to the three kids. The second I did that the ringleader made a quick movement toward my window. I stopped my car and quickly opened my door, which caught the doofus right in the face, knocking him to the ground. I jumped out with my handcuffs and placed him under arrest while my wingman placed the other two under arrest. By this time the other two had gone mute. They were scared out of their minds and didn't want any more trouble. Wish I could say the same for the ringleader.

As I stood him up in cuffs, he began to get tough. Probably because he knew he couldn't go anywhere or do anything. He started saying things to his friends and then he looked at me.

"You're nothing more than a nigger cop. If you didn't have that badge and gun, I'd whip your ass."

I smiled. "Really?"

I could read people, and I could read him. His mouth said one thing, but his eyes and body language said something entirely different. Since I had to work, I might as well have some fun.

Our cruisers didn't have cages like city cruisers, so I placed him in my front passenger seat, seat-belted him in and we headed back to Troop K where I'd have to process him. My wingman transported the other two in his cruiser. Luckily, they were harmless and caused no problems during their transport.

As we drove to the troop, I started to have fun with "Sir talks-a-lot." I turned up my music, took my tie off and started humming the theme from the movie Rocky. I told him that he was going to get a shot at the title, because when we got back to the troop I wanted to see if he was all talk.

He started to sink further and further into his seat. His will was already broken, but I wanted to teach him that he should always watch what he says and to whom he says it because words can come with consequences. We got back to the troop. Before I got out of the cruiser, I turned to him and asked, "Are you ready?"

He didn't respond. He wouldn't look at me. It was hard not to laugh, but I stayed in character.

We went inside and I placed him into the holding cell. I told him I'd be right back.

I secured my gun and thought about what I was going to say to this guy.

I walked into the processing area where bigmouth was being held. "Ready to kick my ass?"

His mouth barely moved but he was able to push out the word, "No."

"You sure?"

I had no intentions of giving him a shot, but I was curious to see what he'd say.

"In the future," I said, "You should watch what you say to people. If anybody calls your bluff, you'll have to be prepared to back it up."

He didn't respond.

"Since you're being calm and non-combative now, I'm going to take you out of the holding cell and process you."

He nodded.

I opened the cage, and the processing began.

After he heard what this guy said to me my sergeant came into the processing room and ordered him to be held on a bond and placed downstairs in lockup. My sergeant was an old school white dude who had no patience for any type of racist remarks by anyone. The ringleader's two friends had already been released and were probably home counting sheep.

Later that night I went down to lockup to check on him. He was lying on this cold- ass metal bed with no blanket. I asked him if all this was worth it. He said no, and that the only reason he was acting like that was because he'd been drinking and that he was trying to show off for his friends.

"What about calling me a nigger cop?" I asked.

He had no response other than he was sorry.

I was getting used to such treatment by the white community I was protecting, but I wouldn't let that stop me from doing my job. It wasn't easy, though.

The next day my sergeant read my report and asked why I gave him so many chances before arresting him. I told him that until the cuffs go on there's always talking to be done. I thought I could spare him and his friends from getting arrested and having that on their record. Maybe it was naive of me to think that they deserved a chance but if you arrest everyone without empathy or understanding then why be a cop. Wouldn't you want a chance not to be arrested if you could?

Chapter 13
EVERYONE LINE UP

It was the early 1990's. By this time, I'd pulled over enough cars to feel comfortable while still being safe.

Being safe doesn't mean pulling a car over, giving out a ticket, and being able to get back in your car in one piece. Being safe means being able to pull a car over while making sure your surroundings are clear of danger and that the car you're pulling over is in a safe location to protect the driver and his or her passengers from oncoming traffic. You have to account for the traffic whizzing by at high rates of speed. You have to be able to observe everything from the trunk of the car you pull over all the way up to the doors.

People wonder why cops check the trunks of cars they pull over. You never know if someone is hiding in that trunk to ambush you as you walk up. It sounds crazy but it's been known to happen. You have to make sure there isn't a second car coming up behind you to take you out while you're dealing with their accomplice who's in the car you just pulled over. The list goes on and on.

If you ever hear someone say that all state troopers do is pull over cars, he or she obviously has no idea what the hell they're talking about. When I'd hear that from people, I'd ask them to close their eyes and imagine that it's two in the morning and the car they pulled over on the highway is stolen and three males exit that car and approach you. What are you going to do? Don't forget that your backup is ten minutes away. Sometimes, after giving them that scenario, they'd look at me and say, "But how often does that really happen?"

I'd smile and say, "Enjoy McDonald's. You wouldn't survive as a trooper."

There's something a lot of cops do that I never felt was necessary, and that's to always have your hand on your gun as you approach a car. I'm not saying I never did it, but when I'd do it, it was because I saw or felt a threat.

I've seen police officers make it a habit regardless of the presence, threat, or even hint of danger.

If you always have your hand on your gun when you're approaching a car and the sudden introduction of stress appears, the first thing that happens is you become tense. When you tense up with your hand around your gun the next thing you want to do is pull it out. This is why some cops make mistakes and shoot people they shouldn't.

I've been pulled over before while off duty in my own car and almost every time the cop has had his hand on his gun. As a Black man you can't help but worry that you might become the next statistic.

Even though I'd pulled over a lot of cars at this point I hadn't really encountered anything out of the ordinary. I had my share of car stops that resulted in the seizure of drugs, guns, drivers with warrants, and even stolen cars, but none resulted in anything more than arrests. I'd also investigated my share of domestic-violence cases and motor-vehicle accidents. And of course, there were your occasional loud noise complaints. All in all, everything was what I'd imagined.

However, during that time in the early 90's the street gangs were in full force in the cities of the Northeast—in particular, Hartford, CT—and they were way out of control.

Hartford is Connecticut's capitol. It's a relatively small city, but it has its share of Connecticut's drug trade. Hartford has your blue- and white-collar workers and in many ways reminds me of New York City, just a lot smaller.

The Hartford Police Department had been investigating these gangs that were very structured and organized and were responsible for most of the drug business and violence in Hartford. These street gangs were mostly comprised of young Black and Latino men and women.

The gangs were vicious and had no regard for human life. People were afraid to walk down the streets, afraid they'd become victims of a gang initiation or a turf war. The streets were a dangerous place to be. If you were a kid, it was worse. You played outside with the fear of catching a stray bullet meant for a rival gang member.

There were so many of them that the Hartford Police Department (HPD) didn't have the manpower to combat them, so they asked for help.

HPD had constructed a task force in conjunction with the state police. Their only objective was to patrol the city streets, identify gang members, and make arrests when necessary. The operation called for members of the state police to be paired with Hartford police officers.

They knew the city and the places hardest hit by these gangs. Strength in numbers and visibility were the keys to a successful operation.

This task force was brought to my attention by my sergeant, who specifically asked if I'd be willing to join. I knew I was being asked not because I was knowledgeable in gang activity or because I was a seasoned veteran, but because I was Black, and most of the gang members were either Black or Latino.

I didn't care what the reason was. It made sense and it gave me the opportunity to learn about street gangs up close and personal. I agreed. Besides, it was a change of pace from the monotony of working midnights in the country.

I'd be remiss if I didn't say I was a little nervous. What you see in the movies is nothing like the real thing. In real life there are no second chances. You get shot; most likely you die. Cops are targets for gangs, which heightened the level of concern. It added a level of danger to my job I hadn't expected, but I was one who never backed down from a challenge. I thought if I could make a difference in this task force, then when it was time for me to move on to a different unit within the department, I'd be better prepared.

I arrived at the Hartford police station for the first day of briefings. We sat and listened to different levels of management explain what their expectations were for this interagency operation and what their end goal was, which was to try to dismantle or otherwise control these gangs so that the violence would cease.

As I looked around the room, I saw some familiar faces. I wondered who I'd get paired with. They called out a trooper's name then they called out a local officer's name they'd be with. My partner ended up being a white officer who knew his stuff and knew the streets.

Sometimes there's animosity between state and local officers for whatever reason, but none existed between us. He first drove me around the city, showing me all the hotspots where the gangs usually congregated and showing me what to look for when trying to identify them. I felt like a kid in school again, taking it all in.

After the initial, get-to-know-the-city drive he showed me all the spots to eat, and we definitely did that. During one of our breaks, he went so far as to take me backstage at the local arena during an En Vogue concert. This city policing was much different from what I was used to.

Now, what would this detail be without a little controversy? A few of my fellow troopers, who were also assigned to this task force, told me they'd heard there were some racist cops assigned to this detail, and that I should keep my eyes open. I've always had to keep my eyes open for that possibility, but I didn't let it consume me. I'd deal with it when or if it happened.

We'd been working various shifts, some days and some evenings, but on this day, we happened to be working the evening shift, when crime was at its peak. My new partner and I had been on a few calls and stopped a few cars throughout the evening. We decided to drive around and be visible. As we engaged in conversation, his police radio gave off this horrendous beeping tone. I didn't know their dispatcher's lingo, but I could tell by his reaction that a situation was happening. He ended by saying, "Ten-four. We're responding."

I didn't know what we were responding to, but it seemed like the situation was under control because we weren't using lights and sirens. He explained that some other officers in our task force had a bunch of suspected gang members detained. I was ready to go. I was interested in seeing how they did things in the city.

We arrived at the scene. Approximately ten young Black males were lined up next to each other, on their knees with their legs crossed and their hands on top of their heads. There had to be at least ten to fifteen police officers, including my partner and me.

The situation was under control, so I moseyed over to where a few of my state-police comrades were congregating and said hello. As we were talking, I had my eyes on the guys who were kneeling on the concrete in case something stupid happened.

If you've ever been on your knees on a hard surface for a long period of time you know that it can get very uncomfortable. One of the local officers, who was white, told the group of Black males not to move. There wasn't anywhere for them to go or anything they could have done with the amount of police presence we had, but sometimes you have to reiterate things so there's no doubt.

A few minutes went by. One of the kids uncrossed his legs so he could readjust himself and then crossed his legs back. I didn't think anything of it but that same white Hartford cop who'd initially told them not to move darted over to that kid like he just said something about his mother. The cop jumped in the face of this kid and said, "Nigger didn't I tell you not to move!?"

I didn't know how to process what I'd just heard. I was in denial. I said to myself there's no way this idiot could be so cavalier, saying that in front of all these police officers, some of whom were Black.

I looked over at a trooper friend of mine who happened to be Hispanic, and we both had the same look on our face. My surprise changed to anger. My immediate desire was to approach him and confront him in front of everyone. As I processed my thoughts, I realized that doing so, at that particular time, would make matters worse. There were still ten suspects on their knees, and I didn't want the situation to get out of hand.

The strange thing was that none of his fellow local officers said anything to him. I knew at that point it was something they were either okay with or opted to ignore. Either way, it wasn't good by me.

There were two sergeants, one from each agency, on the scene. I calmly walked over to the state police sergeant, who was Black. I know he'd heard what I'd heard, and I told him point blank that I was leaving, that I would not stand there and let that officer use such a racial and derogatory slur, nor would I sign any paperwork related to this investigation. I was willing to get written up if need be.

He let out a long sigh and said, "I understand."

I walked toward my partner and told him we needed to go. He didn't ask any questions, he just said OK. We got into his cruiser and drove away.

Black Behind the Shield

When we were in his cruiser I never asked if he'd heard what I heard. Part of me didn't want to know. If he did hear it and was OK with it, then that was a problem. I was still relatively new on the job, so I tended to tiptoe through some things. I knew I had to look myself in the mirror, and if I couldn't do that then the whole reason I'd become a trooper would've been for nothing.

Sometimes in life you're presented with options and sometimes it's the option you choose that will define who you are. Like my mother always says, everything happens for a reason. This situation had to happen early in my career. It helped me understand that it wasn't just the racist people I'd have to deal with in the community, but, increasingly, I'd have to deal with racist people in law enforcement too. How can you combat racism when some of the very people who swore to protect you are racist?

A few months later my time in that interagency task force came to an end and I was sent back to my troop to resume my duties. I learned a lot about gangs and the violence they perpetrate. I also learned how to be more aware of my surroundings due to the fact that a gang member could approach me from any angle at any time. It was a humbling experience, but a necessary one.

Chapter 14
I'M GONNA GET THOSE NIGGERS

When you're a trooper you do everything you can to keep people safe and to enforce the law, and you do so with the utmost discretion and empathy. Not everyone you encounter will immediately give you the respect you deserve. Sometimes you have to earn it. Then there are those people who, no matter what you say or do, hate you. Maybe it's because they don't like cops or maybe it's because they don't like Black cops. Either way, it's an officer's duty to be impartial and handle the situation with an unbiased attitude. Not everyone has to go to jail, but sometimes it's unavoidable.

One fall evening at about 11:30 p.m., it was the usual condition in the Northeast eight or nine months of the year—chilly. I got ready for work every night the same way. I made sure my uniform was sharp and that all the lights, my siren and my police radio were operational in my cruiser. If some of your equipment isn't working, the only thing you'll have to rely on is hope and chance, and when you're by yourself that isn't enough. Sometimes those items can be the difference between life and death.

As a trooper you don't have the benefit of having backup at your disposal like most local police officers do. Troopers ride alone and their backup can be ten, sometimes fifteen, minutes away. That's a lifetime to survive if you're getting your ass handed to you on the side of a road. In any situation you get into, you must consider that you'll be alone for at least that period of time. That includes a combative individual resisting arrest. If you can't picture what that's like, try all-out wrestling with a friend of yours for one minute straight. That'll give you an idea of how tough waiting ten to fifteen minutes for backup is.

With all my equipment working, I made that long trek to the barracks.

Our shifts began the minute we got into our cruisers. I saw some motor-vehicle violations on the way but none too egregious, so I let them slide. As I continued driving, a trooper on the radio said he'd just stopped a car while off duty. The state police in Connecticut are allowed to use their cruisers on and off duty. That's why he was able to stop that car. Their cruiser is what most troopers use 24-7-365, or until they realize that using it off duty can be a headache.

This off-duty trooper had his family with him. On top of that the driver of the car he stopped was suspected of driving while intoxicated.

I wasn't going to let him handle this motor-vehicle stop by himself. He was off duty, and he was with his family.

I responded on the radio that I'd head to the trooper's location. I turned on my lights and sirens and went to assist him.

When I arrived, the trooper's cruiser was parked behind a light-colored four-door sedan. The trooper and I met at the rear of his car, and he explained why he'd made the stop. The driver of the car was a white man, and the passenger was a white woman. I told the trooper he could head home; I'd handle the rest from here.

As I walked back to my vehicle the trooper drove away. Dispatch advised that a trooper from another barracks would be coming to assist me.

This was all taking place on a stretch of highway patrolled by another troop, so the trooper coming to back me up would end up being the person taking control of the situation.

As I waited for the other trooper to arrive the female in the car was moving around a lot. I backed my cruiser up a little bit in case it was more than agitation. Soon after, the other trooper arrived.

I knew this trooper. He was one of the Black troopers I'd graduated with.

I explained the situation. He told me he was going to give the driver a series of field sobriety tests to determine if he was safe to drive. My job was to keep an eye on the female passenger while the trooper conducted his business.

We cautiously walked up to the car and the other trooper escorted the driver to the shoulder on the side of the highway. We could smell alcohol on the breath of both the man and the woman, but the trooper couldn't arrest him based on that, so he continued with the tests.

The female passenger was not having any of it. She started screaming, "You can't do that. Leave him alone!"

I told her politely but firmly, "The sooner you shut the hell up, the sooner we can be done."

Okay maybe it wasn't the politest way to explain this.

"Fuck you!", she screamed!

With a condescending smile I told her to relax.

As I glanced over at the trooper to make sure his tests were going smoothly, the female scooted over to the driver's seat, jumped out the door and bolted into the middle of the highway. I said to myself, "This bitch is crazy."

It was almost midnight so there weren't many cars around. I ran into the middle of the highway, bear hugging her from behind so I could drag her back to safety.

When I got her to the shoulder of the highway, the trooper and I looked at each other and nodded. They were both going to be under arrest.

He arrested the male and placed him in his cruiser. I arrested the female and placed her in my cruiser. Both suspects were handcuffed, as was standard procedure with an arrest. The plan was for me to follow the trooper to his barracks so both suspects could be processed. The male would be processed for DWI, and she was probably going to be charged with interfering with the police, or simply translated, for being a stupid ass.

As I traveled to the other trooper's troop, the female started to kick my police radio, kick me, and kept yelling at the top of her lungs. Because we didn't have cages separating the back seat from the front, she had to sit up front near me, which gave her the opportunity to assault me. The only thing holding her back was the seat belt, which she was trying to undo as she was kicking me.

I radioed dispatch that I was having problems with my female passenger. They advised me that they were going to send assistance. The other trooper had his focus on the guy he was about to transport, so I had to handle the situation on my own until assistance arrived.

I couldn't drive being kicked at the whole way, so I stopped my cruiser and went to the trunk. I had to be quick before she was able to undo her seatbelt. In the trunk was a rope that I had for exactly this type of situation. I was taught in the police academy to take a rope, place it around the ankles of the combative person, make a knot and place the knot outside the door so when the door closes over the knot it keeps the legs from moving. I did exactly that and it worked like a charm. She then started to spit at me. It took everything within me not to back-slap her.

As I was trying to get control of the situation the trooper sent to assist me arrived. He was white.

The minute she saw him she began to calm down. I chuckled on the inside. When she saw this other trooper was white, she immediately felt protected.

I transferred her to the other trooper, told him good luck, and off I went to finally start my shift thinking that was the end of that. It was only the beginning.

The next night I was finishing up my shift and getting ready to head home when the sergeant on duty stopped me in the hallway. He said he heard about the incident I'd had the night before.

I laughed and told him, "It was crazy but it's all good."

He looked at me and said, "You might have some trouble because of that incident."

"Why"?

He begrudgingly told me the woman was filing a complaint for sexual misconduct.

"Who is she filing the complaint against?"

"You and the other trooper."

"WHAT!?"

The sergeant had no more information but said I'd be hearing from internal affairs soon.

I was in utter shock. When he said the words "internal affairs," I knew this was serious.

The 30-minute drive home felt like ten hours. I knew people could be vicious sometimes, but never in a million years would I have thought I'd be on the receiving end of such a bold-faced untruth.

When I got home, I got undressed and sat on my bed thinking about how this happened. Did I do something to provoke this? I couldn't find anything, not one action, that fit this description.

I was dumbfounded so I did what I always did when I was upset or had something on my mind, I called Mom. She always knew how to make things better and could find the reasoning behind certain things. But when I talked to her and explained what was happening, I could hear the fear in her voice. Not because she thought I did something wrong, but because she knew I hadn't and was afraid of what the outcome might be.

I was of a different opinion. The more I thought about it the more confident I became. I'm not the most religious person in the world, but I believed God would make things right.

Several days went by. Internal Affairs contacted me and told me they wanted to meet. Along with my union representative, I headed to their office.

They asked me the same question, just in different ways. My answer was always the same: "I didn't do anything."

They allowed me to read her statement about the accounts that took place that evening. She stated, under oath, that the other trooper and I arrested her and her boyfriend, and that the other trooper placed her boyfriend, while in cuffs, into his police cruiser where he was left alone. Then the other trooper and I took this female in my cruiser and drove away from the highway down a deserted road where we fondled and grabbed her. And we kept doing it until a mysterious police officer showed up and saved her. All the while her boyfriend was still apparently in the other trooper's cruiser alone on the highway.

My reaction: Bullshit!

I looked at the people from Internal Affairs and told them I understood they had a job to do, but her statement didn't even sound believable. Her statement led me to believe this was nothing more than a racist lady's cheap attempt to extort money.

They assured me that was probably the case, but that they had to investigate regardless. I still had to prove my innocence, or my ass was getting fired—or worse. Usually, it's the other way around. They'd have to prove my guilt. Being a Black man, I knew if I left it up to them, they'd somehow find me guilty of something.

This was a time without cell phone cameras, and the only witnesses were me and the other trooper. Things didn't look good for us at all.

I got a phone call from the trooper who eventually transported her that evening. He said he'd heard about the complaint and wanted to tell me about the supplementary report he wrote based on the comments that this female kept blurting out on their ride back to his troop. He said that I'd have to read it because he wasn't comfortable reading it to me. He'd fax me a copy.

I waited anxiously by the fax machine. I was intrigued to read what she'd had to say. The fax machine beeped and spat out several pieces of paper. It almost didn't finish printing before I grabbed the paper from the machine.

I looked it over. "You've got to be kidding!"

She'd made several statements, but what caught my attention was when she said, "I'm going to fix those niggers. I'm going to show them that they can't put their hands on me."

In a strange way I felt better reading it. It showed she was in fact a racist. This wasn't a sexual harassment thing. This was a Black thing.

When someone has that much hate, sometimes they don't realize what they're saying, and to whom they're saying it.

I was thankful for that trooper's wherewithal to notate what he witnessed her saying.

Still, it was internal affairs, and a woman's word against ours. This was like a never-ending nightmare, and

I knew at some point I'd wake up. I hoped that when I did, I was in my own bed, and not a jail cell.

It was several weeks before Internal Affairs contacted me again. They notified me that they had completed their investigation and had concluded there was no merit to her complaint. It was found to be completely false.

Yeah, no shit!

We were ecstatic that we were cleared, and the saga was over. At least, we thought it was. Almost in the same breath that they told me we were cleared, they told me that she was filing a lawsuit against us.

This wasn't just a racial incident. She was out to make some money. She thought her hate for Black people was going to get her paid.

My emotions had run from one end of the spectrum to the other, but I was determined not to let her win. My name was and still is the most important thing I own, and I'll be dammed if I let someone ruin it.

I was prepared to go down swinging. I told the Attorney General's office, which was representing us, that if they gave her one dime to make this go away, I was coming after them. They told me not to worry. But it wasn't their life or reputation on the line.

We got dragged through the mud. Most of the troopers in the department heard about it. Some didn't get the whole story and started to question who we were. It was a horrible feeling thinking everyone believes you did something unethical when you didn't. I was numb with disbelief.

The whole incident had been humiliating but being sent to the medical center so they could take pubic hairs from us to compare with a rape kit they'd conducted took the prize. I truly felt like a criminal.

My mom was a wreck. I kept telling her not to worry. I tried to reassure her I'd be okay even if I didn't totally believe it.

My friends and family stood by me. They knew I was innocent, and their support gave me the strength to stand up to her. Being Black men and having these allegations made against us by a white woman, it was important that we clear our names, not just for us, but for other Black police officers.

The court proceedings began. The first step was to pick a jury. The other trooper and I, on that first day, walked into that courtroom with our uniforms shining and our heads held high. Being in that courtroom however showed us the reality of this incredible and unfortunate situation.

We sat as potential jurors walked in and were called up one by one to be interviewed. As they walked in, the woman who filed this ridiculous lawsuit did not look up once. Her eyes were glued to her kneecaps as she fiddled with her fingers.

I'm guessing she realized we weren't going to cave. We were willing to go to trial to prove our innocence.

After several hours of juror interviews the judge called for a recess and advised everyone to come back after lunch. The other trooper and I went to grab a bite to eat when my pager went off.

I didn't recognize the number, so I used the restaurant's phone to return the page.

It was the Attorney General. He told me we could put our uniforms away. She was withdrawing the lawsuit. It was finally over.

I had thoughts of going after her for defamation of character, but I wanted all this nonsense behind me. We were clear. That's all that mattered.

My career—my life—could have come to an end, and for what? A racist white woman had so much hate she was willing to ruin the lives of two innocent people because they were Black. This whole incident could have gone a totally different way, but we were law-abiding troopers with people on our side who believed in us.

It's not her fault she's a racist. She learned that from somewhere or someone. I don't condone it, but I was taught that you can't control the thoughts and actions of others. You can only try to educate them and help them see that what they're doing, and feeling, is wrong.

My son is a teenager. I've taught him a great deal about life—about drugs, sex, racism, women, and a slew of other topics that relate to his growth as a young man of color in our society.

In our talks, I've emphasized women. They have an unmatched power when it comes to men. I've taught my son to respect them, but to be aware when he's around them. Not that they're bad—I believe the opposite. Women are the most beautiful creatures God made. But most women know they can make any allegation against a man and, unless the man has solid proof to dispel those allegations, the results can be horrendous for the accused, whether he's guilty or not.

Being a uniformed trooper was the pinnacle of law enforcement, but I needed a change. I felt I was a target, being a Black man in uniform, so I had to find another unit where I didn't have to wear a uniform but would still be able to get that action I was looking for.

As I pondered my next step, I thought of this show I used to watch religiously: *New York Undercover*. It was about these two cops, one Black and the other Hispanic, and how they made their living pretending to be different people. It was interesting how they were able to make people believe they were someone they weren't. I always wanted to be an actor, so I thought what better unit for me to be in? It was settled. I was going to apply to be an undercover narcotics detective.

Little did I know that being a target in uniform wasn't half as bad as being a target without.

Chapter 15
THE NEW FACE IN TOWN

The application process to get into the narcotics division wasn't all that tough. I had the blessing of a sergeant I'd previously met. He was already in that division and told me to apply. That sounded like a no brainer to me. Besides, I was a Black man from Harlem going into a division that was made up of five offices that covered the whole state, and there might've been two other Black troopers within the entire unit.

I eventually got accepted and headed to one of the offices that covered the eastern part of Connecticut. It didn't have any Black detectives, but it happened to have the sergeant who told me to apply in the first place.

I was starting a new chapter in my law enforcement career as a narcotics detective. I knew nothing about drugs—what they looked like, how they were packaged, what they cost, or where to find them. My knowledge base was what I saw on TV and the small amount of drugs I'd seized during a few traffic stops. It was like getting picked first for a basketball game because you're Black only for them to find out that you can't play a lick.

They didn't care what I knew. I was the new Black face in town, and they were excited to use me for things they didn't think they could do themselves.

Black Behind the Shield

The reality is narcotics activity isn't a problem that involves only people of color. Society knows this but continues to treat people of color as if we're the only ones involved in the drug trade. As a society we're conditioned to believe that, but the fact remains that all types of people sell and buy drugs. You don't have to be Black to buy from someone Black and you don't have to be white to buy from someone white. It all comes down to attitude. You become an actor.

If you can act like you belong and look like you belong regardless of the people who surround you, people will believe you belong. I've bought drugs while undercover from Black people as well as white and Hispanic people, women, and the occasional grandmother.

Despite why they may have wanted me there, I was up for the challenge of learning a new part of policing. The ins and outs of narcotic enforcement would be another feather in my cap as I continued to learn how to be a complete state trooper.

I arrived at my new office in street clothes because, well, arriving in uniform would have been counterproductive. It felt a little weird. Up to that point, I'd never worked without a uniform. Even though I looked like I was from the streets, I felt like I walked and talked like a cop. I had to make myself realize I wasn't in uniform anymore. I figured it'd be tough at first, but I'd get over it. To be honest, I didn't have a choice.

At my new "home" I met my two sergeants, one of whom I already knew. The other seemed approachable and carried himself with a hint of cockiness, which I took as him knowing his business. If I were going to learn about narcotics, they were the ones who were going to teach me.

They introduced me around the office, and I met some of the other detectives I'd be working with. They, too, were approachable and eager to get me started—with the exception of one. Let's call him "Joe."

Joe was a white detective who appeared to have been there a while. There was something about him that sent my radar up. I wasn't sure if it was the fact that he wouldn't look me in the eye when introduced to me or if it was the "I don't give a crap" attitude he wore all over his face. Either way, there was something off about him. I gave him the benefit of the doubt. I didn't know him yet and had no idea what was on his mind.

There was another new detective who started when I did, and we both needed to be shown the ropes. One of my sergeants asked Joe to drop what he was doing and show us around the area. The sergeant wanted Joe to take us to some of the hotspots to see if we had what it took to buy drugs.

In my head I was like, "Dude, just because I'm Black don't mean I know how to buy drugs," but I took it in stride. I was eager to know if I could do it.

There's nothing like jumping in with both feet, especially when you have no idea what the hell you're doing. We were ready to hit the streets when Joe said in a kind of "fuck you" way that he was too busy, and to have someone else do it.

That old saying, "first impressions last a lifetime" was in full effect that day. I always believed when your sergeant tells you to do something you do it, as long as it's safe and not illegal, but I guess things were different in narcotics. It wasn't that he didn't want to, it was more *how* he said it that stuck with me.

I was set back by Joe's comments, but I still wanted to go out to see the area and attempt to do a little undercover work.

The other new guy and I ventured out on our own, with no backup and no idea where to go or what to do. All we had were our guns and some buy money that our sergeant gave us in case we were able to make a purchase. I was good at thinking on my feet, so I figured I'd go with the flow. Besides, I love acting. This was my time to put my chops to the test.

As we were driving up and down the streets, we came across a neighborhood like mine growing up. There were numerous groups of guys congregating on the corners. I told the new guy, who was driving, to pull up to the next group of guys he saw. I wasn't sure what I was going to say, but something would come out of my mouth. I just hoped it wouldn't be the wrong thing.

I'd be lying if I said I wasn't nervous. This wasn't TV, this was the real deal. My heart was beating so fast I could feel my throat pulsate. We pulled up next to these guys and before I could say anything one of the guys walked over to where I was sitting. I rolled down the passenger window.

"You lookin?"

"Yeah," I said.

He motioned for us to pull to the curb. He came up to the window and asked me how many.

I had no freakin' idea what he was referring to, so I said, "Two."

He handed me two pieces of this white rocklike substance that we later figured was crack, and he told me how much, I handed him the money and off we went.

I couldn't believe it was that easy. As we drove away my heart began to decelerate back to normal. We went back to the office, and I handed my sergeant the two pieces of crack I'd just bought.

He looked at me and said, "You're going to fit in very nicely."

I was proud of myself for going through with it, but it was the kind of adrenaline rush that was exciting but at the same time it wasn't. No matter how many times I did it and no matter what the person looked like, for the first few minutes of each encounter my heart felt like it could be seen beating through my shirt.

From that moment on I was the new guy who could buy drugs. Everyone took advantage of that. When someone had a case and needed an undercover, it was me they asked. It was cool in the beginning, but it had its drawbacks.

I was discouraged from eating lunch in public with the other detectives. The bosses didn't want me to get recognized by the dealers I was buying from. It made sense, but it still sucked. I wasn't handed confidential informants (CIs) to do casework because in the beginning I was relegated to doing only undercover work.

What I did like was that I didn't have to write that many reports. However, when it came to my monthly evaluations I was always called in to the sergeant's office, because I didn't have any self-initiated cases. I respectfully conveyed to him that he couldn't have it both ways. If I were going to be "pimped out" for everyone else's cases then he shouldn't expect me to have my own, especially when I wasn't given any guidance on how to do them. Eventually I had to meet with the unit's commander about this matter. I echoed my same concerns to him.

His response was quick and direct: "He's the sergeant, and he makes the rules, so you do what he says."

The only response I could give was, "Yes Sir."

That was going to be a problem down the line, but I had to worry about the things I could control. I was still getting to know the ins and outs of my new assignment, which I was enjoying. I didn't want that to end.

Being the only Black detective, I sensed uncertainty from one of the sergeants. He started treating me differently from the white detectives, most noticeably the tone he used when talking to me. I wasn't sure why, but it was evident. He'd occasionally make off-color jokes he thought were funny but weren't. He'd talk down to me, constantly questioning me. He made me feel like I was an outsider.

I didn't fret. I was smarter than he gave me credit for. I also had the backing of the other sergeant, the one who got me into the office. But it was stressful. I didn't want to leave a unit that I'd looked forward to getting into. At the same time, I wanted to be treated as an equal, and not just the new Black face in town.

In search of some help, I befriended two white detectives who worked on cases together frequently.

They were knowledgeable in their craft, but most importantly they treated me like an equal and a friend. I became good friends with them and consider them both instrumental in my growth as it pertained to narcotic investigations.

My first real undercover assignment was for one of their cases. Unlike Joe, they took the time to explain every detail of whatever it was they needed me to know and do. Most important, they asked me if I wanted to be the undercover for their cases instead of assuming I would.

Being an undercover is a dangerous job, and to them my safety and concerns for a particular job came first. As we grew closer, they confided in me that they were sure I was detailed to their office because I was Black. It wasn't like I didn't know that, but it gave me confirmation.

These two detectives schooled me to be an efficient and knowledgeable narcotics detective. They gave me examples of how to write search-and-seizure warrants and reports. They taught me how to manage informants. Most of all they taught me that being a detective in a unit such as this comes with a lot of scrutiny, and that I had to be willing and able to listen to people criticize the work we were doing because many didn't understand it.

Because of the work we did, some people on the outside considered narcotics detectives nothing more than an extension of the criminals we pursued. I showed them I couldn't give a rat's behind what anyone else thought. As long as I did my job honestly and by the book, I was good.

Chapter 16
DROP YOUR GUN

In a narcotics unit, the detectives, and officers you work with tend to form a closeness that you don't usually get on patrol. Patrol troopers will work with a group of men and women one day and a different group the next. In a narcotics unit you work with the same people every day. There's a certain camaraderie that's formed simply because you're with the same people all the time. It's a home away from home but without the comforts.

Being that you're together every day, one would tend to believe you'd have an idea of what the people in your office liked and disliked, what they enjoyed eating for lunch, what their favorite color might be. You'd know unequivocally what the people in your office looked like, especially if one of those people were a totally different color and race from the rest.

We had a trooper in our unit who'd been doing several months of undercover work on this big case. That case was to come to an end on this particular day. All the detectives in my office, along with some other detectives from outside agencies, were to assist in the closure of this case. I was excited—this was one of the first big narcotics cases I'd be a part of, and it involved the transaction of a lot of drugs from a drug dealer out of New York City. I hadn't been involved in such a case yet. My objective was to pay attention and learn as much as I could.

I wanted to see how this undercover, and the unit in general, handled this case: how the briefings were conducted, how they set up surveillance, and anything else that would be relevant to me becoming a true and complete narcotics detective.

The learning curve began when the detectives met in a small briefing room where we were brought up to speed on the developments of the case. I was there along with Joe, the two sergeants, and the rest of the detectives from our office.

We received our assignments and were able to discuss those assignments before leaving the briefing room. We'd later have a larger briefing with the other officers and personnel involved in this operation.

My job was relatively simple. I was to conduct surveillance of the area where this operation was to go down and if I saw anything unusual, to call it out. I was still doing some undercover work at that time, so I wasn't going to be involved in any takedowns or arrests, unless absolutely needed. I'd be in a car by myself so I wouldn't be seen with any other officer or detective.

At least, that was the plan.

The goal was to interrupt the sale of a large amount of drugs being brought up from New York by a Black male who was bringing the narcotics to the undercover trooper. The transaction would take place in the parking lot of a supermarket in a town that was predominately white. Black men, no matter where they were from, would naturally stand out.

We geared up and headed to the supermarket parking lot, where we all attempted to find places to blend in so when this guy from New York showed up we wouldn't be seen. When you have three or four cops in a car there's no blending in, but they did their best.

Given my assignment, I was able to freelance. It was nice being by myself. I didn't have to worry about much and could chill until this thing went down. However, it was hard trying to find somewhere to blend in. Like I said, it was a predominately white town. I stood out like a sore thumb. As my dad would say, I felt like a grain of pepper in a sea of salt. But if blending in is what they wanted, then blending in is what I'd do.

I had to be careful. I didn't want to be the one to blow the case. I found a spot to park on the outskirts of the supermarket and had to use binoculars. I'm glad I was there but talk about someone being uncomfortable. Every time someone got within ten feet of my Black ass, I was afraid they might call the cops on me.

We waited for almost two hours before the chatter on the police radio began. Soon I heard one officer say, "I see the target driving in and he's with someone else who's driving a separate car."

The original plan was that the guy from New York was coming by himself.

Most police operations have some sort of wrinkle, but you're trained to iron them out and keep it moving. I wasn't sure how they were going to handle it, but my job was to observe and be backup in case things went south.

South is where this operation appeared to be heading.

The second guy apparently decided to conduct his own surveillance and parked his car away from the first guy. He sat there for a little bit looking around, then he exited the vehicle and began walking towards the supermarket.

In police work you plan for the unexpected. You run through various scenarios in the hopes that, if what you planned doesn't happen, at least you'll still feel prepared. But on this day a second guy going into the supermarket was one scenario they didn't plan for.

I waited in my spot to see what their decision was when my name came over the radio, along with some chatter and some indecision over what to do about the second guy. There was a little pucker factor happening, but I kept my cool and listened.

On the radio, one of my sergeants was requesting—more like telling me— to go into the supermarket, blend in, and keep an eye on the second guy.

My initial thought was, "Are you crazy"?

It wasn't that I didn't want to do it, it just didn't make sense. Yes, he was Black, but in two hours I hadn't seen one person of color exit or enter that supermarket. I'm quite sure the other detectives and police personnel saw the same thing, so why not send a white officer inside? He/she would've had a better chance of blending in. This was a case of "Because you're Black and he's Black."

It wasn't my operation nor was it my decision, so I said, "Roger," and did what I was told to do.

This is the incident I opened the book with. You know how that went.

Black Behind the Shield

My anger at Joe subsided quickly. I actually felt bad for him. It wasn't something he intended to do, and he felt horrible about it. But I had to let him know how I felt there on the scene before the bosses laid into him.

When I approached him outside the supermarket, Joe's face was beet red, and he was remorseful. I told him I accepted his apology, but that he had to be more aware of his surroundings. He could've changed both of our lives forever. I also expressed my concern about him not being able to identify that it was me. I let him know if he'd paid more attention to me, it would probably never have happened. If he reacted to the situation instead of the color, then maybe—just maybe—he could've seen it was me.

He later admitted to me that all he saw was a Black guy holding a gun. He didn't recognize my clothing, or me, nor did he see the cap I was wearing backwards displaying the word "Police."

Some police officers see a Black man and don't think before they act. I'd like to believe our outing in the supermarket taught Joe to be cognizant of that. It taught me that I'm not immune to being racially profiled by civilians or other cops. I had to take extra steps to protect myself. It was unfortunate, and almost deadly, but that's the way it was, and still is.

The impact of that incident didn't hit me until I was alone in my car. I took a minute to reflect on what had happened. I could have died at the hands of someone I worked with. That made me uneasy. But because it involved someone I knew, I dealt with it, made my feelings known, and kept it moving.

Some might say Joe was justified. My back was to him, and he probably hadn't seen the word "Police" on my cap. He was looking at my gun and was under the stress of the situation. I can understand that reasoning, but the problem with that line of thinking is that he had more of an opportunity to assess the situation. My back was toward him, which gave him time to identify me as his coworker and not a suspect. He had ample time to observe the word "Police" on my cap. What's more important, I worked with him every day, and entered the supermarket with him. The situation could've been avoided simply by his seeing instead of only looking.

The incident heightened my awareness toward not just white people, but also toward white cops as well. I never wanted to feel like that, but they'd given me no choice. It was a matter of when, not if, this type of situation would happen to me again.

Chapter 17
NOT AGAIN

Most Black men in America, if not all of us, spend a lot of time wondering if today will be the day we get accused of something we didn't do—or worse, die by the hands of a police officer who doesn't like us because of the color of our skin.

Being a Black man in law enforcement didn't stop me from wondering the same thing. When Black cops get pulled over by white cops, our fear is no different. The only difference is that cops know the tricks of the trade when it comes to racial profiling, so Black cops can tell if that's the case.

I've been racially profiled before. In some ways the experience is worse because, when the officer who conducts the stop realizes I'm in law enforcement, their attitude changes. That's because they knew I was aware of exactly what they were doing.

Many white officers are scared to deal with Black people, and their only course of action is violence. When you have a scared cop dealing with a scared individual, that's a recipe for disaster.

It was becoming clear to me that being Black and trying to do my job was not easy. I was a professional, so I dealt with it. However, I learned over time that no matter what I did on the job, how I did it, when I did it, or why I did it, I was going to be questioned. I always stayed true to myself and continued being the best version of me on and off the job. I wasn't perfect, but I made it a point each and every day to learn from my mistakes and from the mistakes of others.

I was the kind of cop who never liked to talk shop when I was off duty. Everything I did off-duty was purposely not related to law enforcement. I needed time to decompress from all the stresses that came with being a cop.

One way I did that was to play football. Before I entered college, I was in a two-hand-touch football league in Central Park in Manhattan, and I loved it. I continued to play with that team while I was with the State Police.

One Saturday afternoon a friend and I decided to travel down to the city so we could play in this much-anticipated match-up against one of the more competitive teams in our league. There we were, two brothas chillin' and boppin' our heads to some early 90's R&B. The drive down was smooth and uneventful. It was the drive back that was the problem.

We'd been procrastinating leaving for home. We'd just won and were enjoying our victory, but we had to head back soon: my friend had plans that evening. We said our goodbyes to my friends and began the trek back to Connecticut.

On the interstate, in an effort to get home quicker, I did what most people do: I put the pedal to the metal. Being a cop, I was used to driving fast. I'd been trained to do it safely, so I had no worries about getting us home in one piece.

Black Behind the Shield

We were making good time. I assured my friend I'd get him home so he wouldn't miss what he had going on. We entered Connecticut and were bullshitting about nothing in particular, just enough to keep me unaware of this Connecticut trooper sitting in the swale of the highway.

As I passed him, my initial thought was maybe he didn't see me. That was the civilian in me. The trooper in me knew damn well he was gonna come after me.

As sure as the sun was going to rise in the morning, the trooper flipped on his red and blue lights and his siren.

He pulled out and started to pick up speed. There was no question he was coming after me, so to make it easier, I pulled over and waited for him to catch up. I told my friend to remain calm and we'd be on our way shortly. I figured once I showed him my license, registration, and police credentials, I was either getting a ticket or I'd be allowed to leave. Either way the traffic stop shouldn't take very long.

The trooper flew up right behind me, almost coming to a screeching halt. I didn't think that was necessary, I'd already stopped, but to each his own.

After a few seconds his car door slammed, and he approached the passenger-side window. I rolled it down, to make whatever conversation was going to take place easier.

Knowing how Black men are viewed, especially during a traffic stop, I made sure our hands were visible and my interior light was on. I'd grab my information after he came up to the window.

I was about to greet the Trooper but instead of seeing his face I saw the barrel of his gun pointing across my friend's face and into mine.

"LET ME SEE YOUR HANDS!" he shouted.

Everything happened so quickly that I was in shock. My friend immediately put his hands on the dash. I thought, "Not again!"

The Trooper, who was white, was agitated. I could hear it in his voice. He continued to ask for our hands to be visible, which they were. My shock soon turned to anger.

"What the fuck is your problem!?" I yelled, looking right into his eyes. "Why do you have your gun pointed at me? I'm a trooper and I have my badge and I.D. But I don't want to get it while your finger is on the fucking trigger!"

"You're a trooper?"

I told him I was reaching for my badge and ID, which I did slowly. I showed it to him. He holstered his gun.

Once he put his gun away, I couldn't hold back. I went on a tirade. And during this tirade I asked him why he took his gun out in the first place. His response was that I had my foot on the brake, so he thought I was going to drive away.

"Are you kidding me!? You were going to shoot me because I had my foot on the brake!?"

It didn't stop there. I told him if he was going to be scared of two Black guys in a car then he needed to find another profession.

I had a few more choice words for him before I slammed on the gas, screeched my tires, and sped off while he stood at my passenger window. Part of me wanted him to stop me again. The second time it wouldn't have been a conversation. But I was sure he wouldn't, and I'm glad he didn't. It wouldn't have worked out well for either of us.

After I drove away my friend looked at me and said, "I think I shit myself!"

We both started to laugh. However, we both knew how close we'd come to being a statistic.

We made it to my friend's house. I dropped him off, went home, and had a chance to think about the whole incident.

My friend was probably thinking he was going to decline my next offer to drive to the city.

The actions of that trooper reconfirmed once again that prejudice exists not only with civilians but also amongst police officers. My driving off like that wasn't the best move to make, but I was tired of being on the other end of a white cop's gun. When you keep getting targeted and treated like a criminal when all you're trying to do is be Black and live, your actions may not always be rational.

Today, when Black people protest and act out, it's not because they like to, or have nothing better to do. They're tired and frustrated from not being listened to, and from being targeted.

Chapter 18
PUCKER UP

As a narcotics officer you execute search warrants as often as most people change their clothes. You plan and then you plan some more and no matter how much you plan you never know what to expect. The only thing you can expect is the unknown.

Every search warrant is unique, but each has the same variable: Bad guys equal danger. How grave is the danger? It's unknown. Every time I'm standing on that stairwell or on that porch waiting to make entry, the only thing that's going through my mind is "What the hell is behind that door?" The "pucker factor" goes from 0-60 in 2.5 seconds. Okay maybe I'm thinking of the Bugatti Veyron Super Sport, but you get the idea.

All of our state police narcotics offices would occasionally be requested to assist other agencies, whether they were local or federal, with search warrants and other types of investigations.

My boss's boss had notified our office that we were being assigned to assist a federal agency with various search warrant executions. When the feds request assistance from an outside agency, it's usually a "hush-hush" type of deal. You don't find anything out until you arrive that day. I guess they were always paranoid about information leaking. I didn't know the details other than be at point A at a specific time and don't be late.

We had to arrive at the staging area around 4 a.m. It was dark and I still had sleep in my eyes but had to wake up quick. We had to be on our toes come game time. I had to drive to the central part of Connecticut, so I had to get up before 3 a.m. The things I do for my country.

As I made my trek to the depths of central Connecticut, I wondered what the search warrant entailed and what our job was going to be. I'd have the answers to my questions soon enough.

I arrived at the designated location. There was a sea of police cruisers from several different neighboring towns and undercover cars of every make and model. As I looked for a parking spot, police officers could be seen testing their strobe lights on their cruisers and loading shotguns and automatic weapons. I knew one thing for sure: this operation was very big, and very serious.

A loud deep voice could be heard coming from the doorway of the building where we were to brief, instructing everyone to come inside. We were about to receive our assignments.

It was a lengthy and detailed briefing, but we got the information that we needed. The who: some high-level drug dealer; the where: this beat-up three-story duplex; the reason: he might be in possession of drugs and/or guns. So much so that the Feds were going to have their Special Weapons and Tactics (SWAT) unit make entry.

Every time SWAT is needed to make entry there's a higher level of danger. It could mean the Feds had received confirmable information that the homeowner/target was in possession of high-powered weapons, or maybe they'd made references to not getting taken alive, or they could have an extensive history of violence.

My job and the job of the members of my unit was to enter after the SWAT team made their entry, which was fine by us.

Our office gathered by our raid van while we checked and double-checked our equipment. We made sure we all had our bulletproof vests on, that our guns were loaded, our police radios were fully charged and that we were mentally prepared for the mission at hand. After confirming everything was good to go, we entered our raid van and followed the long line of vehicles headed to the raid location.

That feeling of restlessness reared its ugly head again as we headed toward the ratty duplex. Regardless of how big or small the target was I could always see that restlessness on the faces of the other detectives in the van. There'd be occasional jokes while en route, but the closer we got to our destination the more serious the detectives became.

The van slowed. Through the windows against the backdrop of the night sky, members of the SWAT team were hanging on the outside of their van, ready to pounce. It was about to get real.

"GO! GO! GO!" echoed from the police radio.

Our van doors quietly opened. We exited as silently as we could and lined up behind the SWAT team. They were lined up single-file and, once we were behind them, they made their way towards the residence. In the quiet of the night, all that could be heard is the SWAT team jogging to the front of the house.

We followed a short distance behind. We didn't want to get in their way, but we stayed close, ready if needed.

The SWAT team arrived at the front of the building and ascended an outside staircase to the house's third floor. We watched from the ground level as SWAT demolished the door with their battering ram and - BOOM! – Simultaneously detonated a flash-bang grenade that was sent into one of the windows of the residence to disorient anyone inside. This was followed by members of the SWAT team yelling: "GET DOWN GET DOWN!"

I'm so glad that it's not me sleeping in that apartment.

The sound of gunfire snapped me to attention.

Automatic-weapon gunfire is a distinctive sound, but we had no idea from our location whether it was the bad guy or members of the SWAT team.

The bursts were loud and repetitive. The shit was real. The situation had just gone to full ass-puckering.

No instructions came from the radio. We weren't sure what to do. None of us on the ground knew what was going on upstairs. One thing we knew *not* to do was run up the stairs and barge through the door. The SWAT team was trained and could handle the situation, but it was incredibly unnerving.

The gunfire lasted for about ten seconds and then, just as quickly as it started, it stopped. There was a long moment of silence and then came the words that every cop on a raid wants to hear:

"All Clear."

We made our way upstairs to the third floor. As I entered, I almost slipped in what looked like blood. I took a second look. Yep, that's exactly what it was.

A trail of blood led from the entrance into the residence. Cops are nosey by nature so we all, for some demented reason, wanted to see who got shot.

The trail of blood led us to the back room. I wasn't sure what I was going to see but whoever it was they weren't going to be in good shape.

I got to the back room and peered inside.

The blood wasn't from a person but a very large and extremely muscular pit bull that the homeowner/target used for protection and was sent to assault the incoming SWAT team. The canine had dragged itself to the back room before it flatlined. I felt bad for the dog, but the SWAT team did what they had to do to protect themselves.

If this had been one of the search warrants that our office usually conducted and we came across a canine of this stature, I don't know if we would've had the firepower to bring that thing to its knees.

The target was arrested and taken into custody, and the job of our office was complete. Other than the dog that didn't survive, no one was injured.

Things like that don't usually happen on a raid, but high levels of danger are possible every time you approach a door. It runs through your mind before you go through, that someone could be sitting there with a weapon, waiting. The outcome would have been severely different.

Black Behind the Shield

Families of cops who do this type of work see so much on television and in the movies that they can't help but worry. I believe if cops can keep work at work, then the stress level of their family members will be minimal. But for many cops, this is easier said than done.

Chapter 19
I JUST WANNA PUTT

One of my favorite pastimes is the sport of golf. I'm an avid golfer but growing up in Harlem that wasn't an option for me, nor was it a priority. It wasn't until I got older that it became a part of my life.

Golfing helped me get away from the politics of work and enjoy being around friends and family. Plus, I find golf extremely relaxing—until you hit your ball into the woods. You get to be one with the ball. Your game depends on no one but yourself. The smell of freshly mowed grass travels throughout the golf course during those early morning tee times. The competition that evolves between players is second to none.

Some people say golf isn't a sport, but I defy you to try to hit this little-ass white ball into a cup about four inches in diameter and 350 yards away. It's not an easy game, but I love its intricacies, and it gets my mind off the trials and tribulations of everyday life.

Golf for me is best played solo, or with someone I enjoy being around. It could be a friend, a co-worker, or in one case, my son, who was nine years old at the time I tried to introduce the game to him. All he liked to do was putt. That's probably because of all the miniature golf we used to play.

I was trying to stay away from playing miniature golf. When I mentioned the word "golf," my little man would ask which miniature golf course we were going to. If I wanted him to go to a real golf course, I'd have to bribe him. He was just like me, so I used ice cream as my bargaining chip, along with a little bit of competition. He and I love competition and we both love ice cream, so we had the perfect combination. It would be a win-win for the both of us and most importantly we'd be doing it together.

We decided we were going to have a putting contest and the loser was going to have to buy the ice cream. His little butt didn't have a job when he was nine, so you know I was paying win or lose. It was more for the bragging rights. Now all we had to do was pick a course. That part was easy.

I had a good friend who owned a golf course not far from where I lived, so we decided to go there. No one would give my son a hard time if I let him drive the golf cart. I just had to be careful that we didn't end up in a marsh, or worse, a pond. We've come close on a few occasions.

On our way to the course, I told him stories that were completely fictional but always ended with him crying tears of laughter. We looked forward to being together no matter what we were doing. He was my guy, and I wanted him to know I had his back no matter what.

When we arrived, an unusual number of cars were in the parking lot. I could see a number of fairways from the lot, and they were all empty, so something else was going on.

As I took my clubs out of the car my son started with, "You ready to lose?"

We went back and forth on who was going to win or lose until we got to the clubhouse where we met my friend who owned the course. We chatted for a bit. He informed me there were so many cars in the parking lot because there was a party upstairs in the restaurant. I thought, cool, we wouldn't have to worry about holding up anyone on the course.

From the first hole he was driving that golf cart like a mad man. He was having fun and I was having a heart attack. I made sure we were safe though. After I played a few holes, I could tell he was getting bored. I asked him if he was ready for our putting competition. That woke him up. He responded with a resounding, "Yeah!"

I took over the driving duties and we headed back to the clubhouse.

My car was parked on the upper tier of the parking lot, so I drove the cart up a small path that led to the upper tier. We returned my clubs to the car, grabbed our putters and a couple golf balls, and we were ready to go.

As we returned to our golf cart, several guests from the aforementioned party had exited the restaurant and were congregating on and around the cart path that we needed to use. I leaned over and told my son we weren't in any rush. We'd wait until there was an opening and then we'd go. He was an easygoing kid, so that didn't faze him. We sat and talked while we waited.

As we talked, more and more partygoers came outside to mingle while holding their drinks. Some of the guests had had a little too much to drink: they were slurring their words and repeating the same thing over and over again. And they were loud as hell.

About five minutes had passed when a lady from the party caught my eye. She gingerly walked over, probably reacting to all the alcohol, and very nicely asked if we were trying to get by. I told her we were, but we weren't in any rush. She and her friends could take their time and we'd pass when it was clear.

"Nonsense," she said. "You don't have to wait."

She called to the people standing on the path to move over so we could drive by. It was like Moses and the Red Sea; they parted down the middle and cleared a path for us. My son and I said, "Thank you," and proceeded to drive down the cart path.

As we passed the entrance to the restaurant where people were still standing a male voice shouted something that sent shock waves through my body.

"Hurry up nigger!"

It took a second to register, but then I stopped the golf cart and jumped out.

This white guy was standing by the edge of the cart path staring at me.

"Were you talking to me?"

"You heard me nigger. Hurry up."

I was taught the "sticks and stones" saying, but this wasn't one of those times. I've always believed that if you want to disrespect me that's one thing but when I feel you've disrespected someone in my family—in this case, my son—then we've risen to a whole different level. This was personal.

I started to approach this drunken fool at the same time he started to approach me. As soon as I took my first step towards this idiot, three of his friends tried to hold him back. His first step was slow but as soon as they started restraining him, he became more belligerent and combative. I guess his beer muscles started to kick in.

I stood there and told his friends, "Let him go." I was prepared to do whatever had to be done.

He continued with the racial slurs. I continued to stand my ground, waiting for his friends to release him.

Another guy walked up to me. He approached me with his palms facing me to show he didn't want any trouble.

"I'm sorry for my friend, he's a little drunk."

"Don't give a shit," I said, as my eyes remained on the drunken fool.

"Listen, I'm in the military so..." Not wanting him to finish his resume I responded with impatience.

"Quite frankly your background doesn't impress me. I'm with the state police. After I kick your friend's ass he's going to jail."

I guess my state police background out-trumped his military one.

He turned to his friend. "Dude, let's go before you get arrested."

As he kept trying to relay that message to an obviously hardheaded individual, I looked over my shoulder to where my son's little face was peering at me. My body went limp from disgust.

This nine-year-old little boy, who looked up to me, was ingesting every word and every action of mine. I was heartbroken.

I turned away from my encounter with the idiot squad and made a beeline back to my son. I sat in our golf cart, put my arm around him and we headed down to the putting green.

During that short trip I was thinking about what I was going to say to him that would explain my actions as well as the other guy's actions.

We stopped in front of the putting green, and I turned to him.

"I'm so sorry."

I apologized to him for getting out of the cart and leaving him sitting there without any explanation. I apologized for almost getting into a physical altercation with this dude. I explained to him that it had to be done, that there will be times in his life that he has to stick up for himself as well as others. I let him know I was sticking up for him for the disrespect that the guy displayed towards him as well as me. I told him that I could've kept driving the cart and acted like I didn't hear him, which would have avoided the entire situation, but people like that must realize that they can't say whatever they want to people.

Yes, I stopped because I felt he was being disrespectful, but was it right? I reminded him that as long as I was alive, I'd stand up for him no matter what the cost and no matter how bad the ass whuppin. A good friend of mine asked me if I'd react the same way again knowing what I know now and my response to him was… "I don't know."

We are all human, and sometimes things affect us and make us react. I told my son that being drunk is not an excuse for racism. The things you say and do all have consequences. I explained that, if I'd gotten into a fight, even though I was protecting him, I would have had to deal with the consequences, whatever they may have been.

"Did you hear that guy call me a nigger?"

He looked at me with the most innocent of looks and said he did.

I explained to him that, as a young man of color, it might've been the first time he heard it, but it wouldn't be the last. He had to know that it wasn't a matter of "if" but "when" he'd be called that to his face. How he handled it would define him. I told him it's okay to walk away, but it's also okay to stand up for what you believe in.

I looked into his motionless face and asked him if he understood what I was trying to explain. Without hesitation he told me he did. In a weird way I could tell by his demeanor that he was proud I stood up to that guy. It was a learning moment for both of us, and it brought us closer together. I wish it never happened but at the same time I'm glad it did. We both grew that day. We're still growing today.

We had our putting competition, and you already know who won. No, it wasn't him. He knows if he's ever going to beat me at anything he's going to have to work for it.

As we headed back to the car my friend, the owner of the course, came running up to me and thanked me. I asked him for what? He said for not plastering the drunk's face all over his parking lot. We laughed and I told him I was sorry for any undue problems I may have caused.

Police officers are faced with situations like that on a daily basis, but according to the public we're supposed to turn the other cheek. What the public forgets is that we're human, and not perfect. In retrospect, I probably should have kept driving the cart past that idiot on that day and ignored the comment, but the human part of me knew I couldn't let that go. It all worked out in the end.

One day that guy will probably try that again with someone else. The outcome could be a lot different.

Chapter 20
POWER

What is power?

When some people think of power they think of the strongman at the circus, or they think of Aaron Judge hitting majestic home runs over the centerfield wall at Yankee stadium, or they may even think of the power of suggestion, but when I think of power it's that ability police officers possess that allows them to do pretty much whatever it is they want.

According to Google, one of the definitions of power reads: "a right or authority that is given or delegated to a person or body."

I think Matthew McConaughey's character Rust Cohle in the HBO series *True Detective* summed up the dark side of police power best when he said, "Of course I'm dangerous. I'm Police. I can do terrible things to people with impunity."

When you graduate from the police academy, that authority is bestowed on you in a way the normal person cannot fathom. Prior to their graduation, whether it's local, state, or federal, most law enforcement officers have no idea the amount of power they're about to possess. For some, it's overwhelming. That's exactly what I went through upon my graduation from the police academy.

My graduation was in late December 1989. That day was surreal. There I was, marching with my classmates into Welte Auditorium on the campus of Central Connecticut State University. With every step we took the misty smoke grew thicker and the military-type music got louder. We were the newest class of state troopers, the New Kids on The Block if you will, and we looked damn good. With every step my chest grew bigger and bigger. You couldn't tell me jack.

As I walked, I could see my mom, sister and other relatives who'd made the long trip through the Northeast snow to be there. I wanted to wave to my mom like I did when I was in kindergarten during a Christmas play, but I was soon to be a big bad trooper, so I had to restrain myself.

My dad was unable to come see me graduate from the police academy. I didn't know why he couldn't make it and I didn't ask, but something had to be keeping him away. I prayed that whatever it was, it wasn't going to get him back in trouble.

Part of why my chest was feeling puffy was the incredible pride I felt after completing seven months of vigorous training, and part of me knew I was gonna be "The man."

They can prepare you for the streets and police procedures, but they can't prepare you for what your mind will be going through on graduation day. We all took our seats and had to listen to speaker after speaker. It took nearly two hours for them to finally give us our badges. That's all I wanted.

They called my name and I marched up to the podium like the tin man with no oil. I stood there as the commissioner pinned my badge on my uniform. As I shook his hand and walked off the stage, I could feel this light beaming all around me. It wasn't a real light—that would have been weird. It was that power I referred to.

I sat back in my seat and thought I was made of steel. I could do anything. I could stop any car for any violation, I could arrest you for anything, and I always had a get-out-of-trouble (notice I didn't say jail) card, which was my badge. At least, that's what I was feeling.

The confidence we all had was overwhelming. For most of us we realized it was just a thing, and we soon came down off that high. The sad part is some couldn't, and that power manifests and grows until it becomes uncontrollable and is unleashed on the public, friends, and worse, their families.

This power can only be handled by certain types of officers—those who are honest, good-natured, humble and want to help their fellow man. Those who are dishonest, bullies and, last but not least, racist, are the ones who use it to hurt people.

I considered myself a decent human being, and I knew I could use my newfound power to do good. But sometimes even good guys have lapses in judgment.

One night I left the house of a girl I was dating. I was mad, and I took it out on the public. I stopped every car I could that night and gave out tickets like Oprah gave out cars. I did it because I could. Even though every car committed a legitimate violation, it was still wrong. I knew this and, after that night, I learned never to let my personal life intrude on my professional judgment.

The bad cop in that situation might use their power to beat, injure and in extreme cases kill because they feel like they can. If you add the fact that the bad cop happens to be racist, then all the senseless acts of violence we've witnessed over the years by these individuals are the result.

Again, the majority of law enforcement officers are made up of great, caring, and compassionate men and women. They joined the force for the same reason I did: to help people and make a positive impact on society. Like any profession, a few bad apples get through the weeding-out process. When one of those bad apples does something inexcusable, it becomes amplified, and makes all cops look bad.

One weekend I picked up my mom from the train station so she could visit with me. I was wearing shorts, a tank top, and sandals, and driving my police cruiser.

As we made the trek to my house on the highway, my mom noticed that every car in front of me kept pulling to the right. Yep, there goes that power again. I wasn't tailgating and I didn't have my overhead roof rack lights attached to the top of my cruiser. It was simply my Ford Crown Victoria with the giant spotlight positioned in front of the driver's side window that gave me away. My mom made a comment that I must feel like Moses and the highway was the Red Sea. (Can you tell I love that analogy?) I did feel kind of like Moses.

As the drive continued, a car cut across from the High Occupancy Vehicle Lane (HOV) into the other lanes of traffic. Me being a trooper, I couldn't stand for that. I had to do something. They'd just committed the crime of all crimes. Ok maybe not, but I still felt like I needed to do something. I was relatively new and still had my power meter on high. I pulled the offending car over.

Before you say it, yes it was the dumbest thing I could have done because 1.) I had nowhere to put my weapon—I was in shorts and a tank top; if something went down, I'd be unable to protect myself, and 2.) I had my mom with me.

I went up to the car, identified myself, and began a short lecture as to why that maneuver wasn't safe. There I was talking safety and walking up to cars in sandals.

When I returned to my cruiser my mom gave me a look as if to say "Why?" I told her I had to; it was my duty.

No, it wasn't. I did it because of that power. I realized that as I drove away from the vehicle. It was a dumb thing to do, and I learned from that.

I mention this not to make me look stupid, even though it did, but to show you that even a good cop, like I believed I was, could be seduced by that power. Some police officers feel a sense of entitlement, and that can seriously cloud an officer's judgment.

Every job and every person has possessed or felt some sort of power. We all deal with it in our own way. Whether it be the power of restraint, the power to heal, the power to fight, or even the power of seduction. If used in the right way, all of these can be amazing gifts. However, each one, if used in the wrong way, can have a devastating effect. If we all used our power to make positive changes, imagine where we'd be as Americans.

Chapter 21
SANDWICH SHOP GUY

Have you ever had an acquaintance that you knew from a store, the library, or even a gas station? Every time you walked into one of those places you knew that person well enough to say hello. But then you're walking down the street and that same person walks up to you but they're not at work, so you don't recognize them. They're out of their element. In your head you're like, "Damn I know this person, but I can't remember where from," but you say hi and either keep talking till you figure it out or you keep it moving.

It's happened to me a lot. I just play it off until my old-ass brain kicks in and I go, "Oh yeah, you're from..." Or "Didn't we...?" Even if I didn't remember, I was cordial and respectful, probably because I didn't want to make a fool of myself, but mostly because that's the way I was raised.

On the job, I ran into tons of people all the time, and trying to remember them wasn't easy. I could barely remember what I did yesterday, and they wanted me to remember someone from a month ago? Please.

As a State Trooper it was about the people, but it was also about the money. That green. Cash. Duckets. Any other synonym you can come up with. The money was pretty good, but there was always room for improvement, something extra I had my eye on. When I wanted to make a little extra cash, I worked highway construction projects or HCP jobs.

These are the kinds of jobs where you see troopers standing by construction sites on the highway directing traffic or just standing there as the cars go whizzing by. I was in the narcotics unit, so the extra-duty jobs I put in for were at night, because I worked my regular shift during the day. It was what they called blood money: those night jobs could start anywhere from 7 p.m. until midnight and go until 6 a.m. and, yes, I had to be back at work later that morning, so a brotha was tired. But I still got my day job done.

One night I was working HCP on I-84 about five minutes west of Hartford. It wasn't a bad job. All I had to do was keep my cruiser lights on so oncoming traffic would slow down and keep the construction workers safe. Like clockwork when 2 a.m. rolled around I got hungry. If I went all night without eating, I wasn't going to be a happy camper come 9 a.m.

The other trooper I was working with told me about a restaurant right off the highway that a lot of troopers frequented because the owner loved cops. I was like, "Cool." I told the other trooper I'd be back shortly.

I contacted a couple of trooper buddies on the radio who were working patrol in the area, and I told them to meet me at that restaurant.

That trooper wasn't lying. When we got there a guy, who I later found out was the owner, came up to us and introduced himself. He told us to sit wherever we wanted, and he'd take care of us.

I wasn't sure what he meant but I had a good idea. Being that I still had an HCP job to get back to I couldn't be there long, so I ordered my food to go.

While I waited, the owner came over and shot the breeze with us. He was a nice, friendly guy. We could tell he liked cops cuz he was all up in the business. His thick accent led me to believe he was originally from Italy.

As we talked a second guy came over. He was white, short, and skinny. I was a great reader of people, and I could tell by his body language and mannerisms that him coming over to say hello was more like, "Hey I need cop buddies in my life in case I get in trouble." It didn't bother me though. He treated me nicely and spoke with respect.

He told my buddies and me he owned a sandwich shop across the street and if we were ever in the area to stop by. Lunch would be on him. I didn't care how many cop buddies he needed; I was eyeing that free sandwich.

I told him I appreciated the offer and that I'd soon take him up on it.

With a big ole grin the owner brought my food to me and said, "Here you go."

I said thank you and proceeded to the cashier, but the owner wasn't having it. He was not going to let me pay for my food. I wanted to leave something, so I left a few bucks on the counter and told him thank you and that I'd be back again.

As I was leaving, the sandwich shop guy made sure to remind me to stop by. I was like, "Damn this dude has it bad for cops." I thanked him and headed back to the construction site to finish my shift.

The next day I was back at work in narcotics, a little tired but ready to do my job. When I worked in narcotics, I always wore something that would help me blend with the street thugs. Often it was my timbs, a hoodie and jeans. In today's society, that's an outfit to get a Black man shot. Rest in peace Trayvon Martin!

Lunchtime rolled around and I decided to check out the sandwich guy's shop to see how it was. I jumped into my undercover whip and headed out.

I got there and it was a little busy, probably because it was lunchtime, duh! I could see the guy I met the night before behind the counter. In an attempt to not look like a stalker, I waved to get his attention, but the dude looked right through me. It was busy so I shrugged it off. As I waited in line to order, I noticed he was being pleasant to the other customers, all of whom happened to be white.

It was finally my turn to order. I approached the guy and said, "Hey how ya doin'?"

He gave me a disgusted look and said, "What?"

"Don't you remember me from yesterday?" I gave him a confused smile. "I met you at the restaurant across the street."

You would've thought he'd have taken a few seconds to try to figure out who I was, but me being dressed the way I was and the color I was, I didn't warrant any extra consideration. I started to tell him I was the trooper he met last night, but he cut me off.

"I don't have time for this. If you aren't going to order, then you have to leave."

"Wow," I said quietly.

I was dressed differently, and he might've had a hard time remembering me, but as a customer I should never have been treated like that. It was rude. I got pissed. He wasn't only rude to me personally; he was rude to a Black man he didn't try to recognize because he wasn't in uniform.

It could have been he was having a bad day, or maybe that he was busy, but his actions were similar to workers of other establishments I've visited where patrons were predominately white, and I was treated rudely.

The moment I'd met him at that restaurant I picked up that something wasn't right about him, and now I knew what it was. I said nothing else. I turned around and left.

That wouldn't be the last time he saw me.

About a week went by. I had the same HCP job, so I decided to go visit my new friend the Italian guy at the restaurant. I went by myself this time and decided to eat my food there. When I got there, guess who was sitting at the counter talking to the owner? Yep, the dipshit from the sandwich shop.

I called the owner over and told him what happened at the sandwich shop. I could see in his face his embarrassment, but he needed to know how his friend treated people. Sandwich-Shop Guy was an indirect extension of the owner, and I didn't want people to think the owner was the same way. I ended the conversation by telling him I didn't want that guy anywhere near me.

The owner was displeased. He welcomed police officers who came to his restaurant, and he didn't want any bad blood between himself and the officers. I sat at a booth while he relayed my message to Sir Dip Shit. I was looking forward to seeing what his reaction was going to be. I needed a laugh and was sure I was going to get it.

The owner and Sandwich-Shop Guy started to talk. The guy wouldn't look in my direction. I hoped I made him so uncomfortable that he pissed his pants.

He took a deep breath and worked up the nerve to walk towards me. Apparently, he hadn't understood my message. As soon as I had eye contact with him, I did my best Mutombo impersonation and with one finger I waved him away.

It was like he hit an invisible wall. He stopped and turned around. I ignored him, ate my food, and headed back to my site, but not before thanking the owner for another lovely meal.

Whether he remembered me or not wasn't the issue. It's how he viewed me when I wasn't in uniform. He treated me like some sort of hoodlum who'd slept with his wife. All because of the way I looked. When I was in uniform however, he wanted to be my best friend. He had a problem with Black people, but not when he thought they could benefit him.

I learned early on: treat everyone with respect until they show you they don't deserve it. When you judge a book by its cover you can miss out on some of the interesting things that book has to offer. Black men and women are no different. Some white people judge us because of what we look like, but if they took the time to put their grievances aside and listen to us, they might be amazed at the things they could learn and at the friends they could make.

Chapter 22
NO MAS

By this point in my career, I'd done hundreds of undercover cases, some fun, some exhausting, and some downright dangerous. I'd seen things the normal person only sees in the movies. I'd been in crack houses packed with people who were shooting, snorting, and smoking every drug you could think of. I'd seen a guy get knocked out cold when trying to purchase crack just because. I've been cornered at a bar by a drug dealer and asked if I was a cop. Talk about a heart-beating-in-your-throat type of moment.

I'd also been in houses where kids were sitting right there watching the whole deal. On a few occasions I'd told the drug dealer I wasn't going to buy if the kids were there, and the dealer's response was "Take it or leave it." Because I wanted to see the case through, I took it.

When you have a family, seeing kids like that starts to get to you. You try to block it out for the good of the case but seeing that time and time again builds up stress. For a police officer, especially an undercover police officer, stress is no good.

Some of these kids would look at me like I belonged there, which was disconcerting. That meant I was one of many who stopped by to purchase drugs from their dad, brother, or whatever relation they were.

Undercover cases weren't all bad. On one occasion, guys from my office did undercover work at a strip club. I was regulated to surveillance... outside. When it came time to execute the search warrant on the strip club, we had more volunteers than normal. Hmmm... I wonder why.

After we entered and secured the bar, another guy and I were assigned to escort the dancers back to their dressing room so they could change clothes. Like I said before, the things I had to do for my country.

There was one case that wasn't so fun. I'd been transferred to a narcotics office that covered the Northern part of Connecticut. One of the sergeants at that office offered me an undercover assignment. Me and two other guys from my office were to assist Liquor Control with bar checks they were going to conduct at a few bars in one of the local towns.

Liquor Control is a department within Consumer Protection. Some of their duties include, but are not limited to, underage drinking and the checking of liquor licenses. We were asked to assist because of the possible drug presence at these bars.

Liquor Control was working in conjunction with one of the local police departments. Our job was simple. We were to go into the bars prior to the arrival of the Liquor Control officers so when they entered, we could observe any patrons who dropped drugs or paraphernalia on the ground. We'd discreetly point them out and then we'd leave. Simple enough.

I arrived for a briefing at this local police department with the other two undercover (UC) officers as well as members from my office. Initially, nothing seemed out of the ordinary. It all sounded pretty easy. I did note that the other two UCs were Black and Hispanic, respectfully. That stigma of being a minority who's asked to do these kinds of assignments *because* you're a minority wasn't going away.

As the briefing continued and everyone was getting their assignments, an officer from this department said that one of the bars we were going to was frequented by gang members. That sent my radar up, but it wasn't anything I hadn't done before.

I liked to get as much information as possible before I did anything, whether it was serving a search warrant, doing an undercover assignment, or buying a car. I asked this officer if he knew that the people going into this "gang" bar would be subject to a pat-down prior to being admitted. I was told very nonchalantly not to worry about it. He didn't believe they did that.

His explanation left me feeling uncertain. All three of us were going to be armed. I asked a couple of the other local officers the same thing and got pretty much the same response. I decided that even though I had concerns, it was probably all good.

It's funny, cops who don't do UC work usually don't think of things like that. Nor do they really care. It's not their asses on the line.

There was always a sense of nervousness because of the unknown of undercover work. But once a few minutes passed, I was in character and ready to go.

Black Behind the Shield

The two bars we started with went off without a hitch. But as we arrived at the third bar, I had a suspicion it would be more of a challenge.

First: more officers were brought in for this bar. Second: we'd already been briefed, but we met up to go over the particulars one more time. The reason became clear—this was the infamous "gang bar."

The other two UCs and I arrived at the bar and parked just up the street from the entrance. We were all in one car and each of us had our state-issued firearms concealed in the waistband of our pants underneath our shirts and jackets. You never know what you might walk into. The surveillance team couldn't park close to the bar. Most of the locals in the area knew most of the cops and they didn't want to be recognized. We were pretty much on our own.

One of the UCs radioed to the surveillance team and advised them that we were about to exit his car and enter the bar. It was nighttime and other than the streetlights, the only lights illuminating the street were coming from the bar. As we walked closer, the music from the place got louder.

At this point all three of us were relaxed. In fact, we were looking forward to going inside to see what it was like.

We walked toward the front door of the bar, scanning the area, making mental pictures of the surroundings just in case things went bad. We wanted to know who was in close proximity, where our exit points were, and who was in the way of those exit points. We were the only pedestrians on the street.

At the front door stood a doorman. Two people were off to the side. One by one we were greeted by the doorman who asked for our identification (I.D.). I was the third in line and I had my I.D. in my hand ready to go. A lot of times doormen don't really look at your I.D., they glance at it to say they did. My name could read Daffy Duck and they wouldn't have a clue.

The first UC had his I.D. looked over and was about to walk into the bar when one of the two people standing off to the side yelled to the doorman, "Yo, I don't know them so check 'em."

The doorman began to pat us down.

Now you know why I kept asking if they pat people down at this bar. If we'd known this or least were told that they might, then we might've decided on an alternative approach. Maybe we would've kept our assess in the car and let Liquor Control do their thing.

Long story short, the doorman found the first UC's gun and we weren't allowed to go in. We didn't argue or linger. You never know what kind of trouble a doorman finding a gun will produce.

We headed back to the car and radioed the surveillance team to let them know we didn't make it inside. We asked them to relay that message to Liquor Control. The second UC and I remained outside the car, bullshitting until the cavalry came.

The first UC was in the driver's seat talking on the radio. He had his passenger side window open so he and I could talk while we waited for the rest of the team. I was leaning in with my arms resting on the car window and the second UC was leaning on a fence behind me when the doorman left his post and walked up the street toward us. I didn't think much of it until he approached the vehicle parked directly behind our vehicle. It still wasn't that crazy, but now I had my eyes on him.

As a police officer you must have the ability to analyze your surroundings and think two steps ahead. I'd scanned the area walking towards the bar, and now I did so again, but with the doorman in mind, as well as the area around him.

The doorman made his way to the trunk of the car parked directly behind ours. I had no idea what he was doing but it wasn't normal.

He opened the trunk slowly, almost as if the trunk lid was going to fall off if he opened it too fast. He stood there for a second, looked over his shoulder toward the bar, then glanced over at us. Something was up. He looked both ways before closing the trunk.

He started to walk back toward the bar when suddenly, he turned in our direction and raised a handgun.

This guy had a gun, and he was coming toward us. *Oh Shit!*

As he sprinted towards the passenger side of our car, I darted to the driver's side and took my gun from my waistband as the second UC quickly ran up the hill away from the commotion. I didn't know where to, because all my attention was focused on the guy with the gun. The doorman went to the open passenger window and with his finger on the trigger, pointed his gun at the UC who was sitting inside.

We're going to have a shootout, and someone might get shot. I just didn't know who.

I crouched down with my gun by the driver's side window. The doorman yelled at the UC in the car. I couldn't make out what he was saying, but it wasn't good. If I hesitated, my friend could get shot.

I thought about shooting the man, but he had a gun pointed at the UC with his finger on the trigger. If I shot him his reflexes might squeeze the trigger and shoot the UC.

The safe play would be to break cover and announce that we were police officers, even though we didn't have our badges with us. I was hoping that plan would buy us a few minutes until backup arrived. I guess I was hoping he'd take our word for it. Yeah, I wouldn't have either.

I was about to yell out that we were the police when a second guy I hadn't seen startled me.

He stood at the rear of our car. I looked at his hands to make sure he wasn't armed.

Where the hell is backup?

The guy standing behind our car motioned with his eyes to the doorman that I was there. I thought, *it's not going to be me that dies tonight.*

I tried to keep my eyes on the second guy while the doorman slowly walked from the passenger side of the car to the front. The second guy hadn't displayed any weapons, so the doorman and his gun garnered all my attention. He walked ahead about ten feet from the car so as to put some space between him and me. He then slowly peaked over to the driver's side of the car.

We locked eyes. Both of us had our guns pointing downward. He started to raise his. I responded in kind. I had nowhere to go and no cover to take. Shooting him was coming down to my last option.

Out of nowhere came the words, "DROP YOUR GUN!"

The street was full of cops pointing their guns. This happened in the blink of an eye.

Because of my previous experiences with mistaken identity and the fact that I hadn't worked with most of these cops before, I lowered my gun. Thankfully, this time, they were talking to the doorman.

He lowered his gun but wouldn't drop it. After one last warning, he eventually dropped it. Everyone swooped in and detained him. The second guy who appeared to be with the doorman must've secretly walked away when the police arrived because he was not to be seen again.

I got thoroughly pissed off. This could have been the end of me. This was different from my other encounters with guns. He wasn't a police officer, he was a civilian, and I really thought he was going to shoot me.

I felt like kicking the living shit out of the doorman. But as a cop, I had to accept that it was all part of the job. The emotions I was feeling had to be put in check.

Once the situation was under control a rush of other emotions hit me. I thought of my beautiful daughter, our eldest child, who was only seven months old then. She came *this* close to losing her father.

I walked to the nearest desolate corner and started to let those emotions out.

As I stood on the corner, my cell phone rang. It was late, so I knew who it was. My wife. For some weird reason she felt something wasn't right and thought she should call me.

I did my best to try to make her believe everything was cool, but she wasn't buying it. I insisted I was fine and told her I'd explain what happened when I got home.

When I got home, I didn't tell her the whole truth. It would've created unnecessary worry.

It was because of the fear I felt in that moment, the fear of my daughter losing her father, that I said, "No more." I remained in the unit but never did any more undercover work. Some cops, things like this don't bother them. But it bothered me. My daughter was the one thing I cared about the most. I wasn't going to let her lose me.

Being a police officer is not an easy job, especially for your family. They worry about you because of the nature of what you do. I always checked in with home and called my mom in New York after working late, just to let everybody know I was safe.

My wife is the daughter of a retired police officer. She dealt with the fear of him going to work every day. Her father was like me in the sense that he kept work at work. But now she was an adult whose husband was a cop and the father of her children. In some ways she was more equipped to handle the stress that comes with being a cop's wife, but at times the worry was more intensified because of the undercover narcotics work I was doing. There was always that possibility when I left for work that I might not come home. If the shoe were on the other foot, I don't know if I could've endured that worry every night.

The other day I asked my daughter if growing up with a cop as a father made her worry. She told me she never really thought about it. That was the response I wanted to hear because I always kept family first. I made it a point to keep work at work so when I came home, I was just Daddy. I didn't talk about work unless there was a funny story to tell. If I was upset about how my day went, I made sure I let it go before I got home. I was all smiles when I walked through that door. My job was to protect them, not to worry them.

My son was younger. I could have worked in outer space as long as I was home on time to play with him. Once I had kids, I put their activities before overtime and before the job. You bring the job home and no matter how you try to hide it; they know.

I had a conversation with a new officer who'd been assigned to our unit. He was wet behind the ears and a hard charger, but a really good guy. Being a cop was his life.

Bedsides schooling him on the procedures of a narcotics officer I also tried to school him on the importance of family. I told him that when he had children, he couldn't let the job run him, he had to run the job. It was important for him to understand that he needed to watch his children grow up. That's hard to do when you devote all your free time to working. I told him it was a great job and I felt blessed to have it, but it never defined me. I was hoping to get that same message through to him.

Like most young guys, he was hardheaded and didn't listen. It wasn't until I retired, and he had kids of his own, that he realized what I'd been trying to say. He called me up to thank me. He told me he looked into his daughter's face and our conversation hit him out of nowhere.

That was one of the best phone calls I ever got.

The incident with the doorman was the beginning of the end for me. The importance of family would play an important role in my decisions going forward, and as long as that remained true, the job would become tougher. It was only a matter of time before an incident would happen to make me say, "I'm done. I'm out."

Chapter 23
NURSE RATCHED

No one likes going to the hospital. If you're there, something's wrong. I hate hospitals, probably because I've spent most of my life in and out of them. I've had a hernia, a torn Achilles tendon, and three knee surgeries, and that's only the tip of the iceberg when it comes to me and injuries. I was in the hospital more times one summer than most people will be in a lifetime. It was so bad that summer that during one of my mother's many hospital visits with me the receptionist asked if she was an employee. She said "No," and gave me a look like "If my kid wasn't so damn reckless…"

I played hard and fell hard, and the hospital was the price I had to pay.

I experienced racism at a hospital, and it was something that caught me off guard. You hear of racism in police departments, stores, restaurants and even golf courses, but when it extends to our hospitals and healthcare professionals, how are we supposed to deal with that? How are we supposed to get proper care if the person assigned to give us said care is a racist? It seems we're always fighting an uphill battle with no end in sight.

I'm someone who has a high pain tolerance. You might hear me say "ouch" every now and then, but I'll never complain about it. If I do, that means something's wrong. I don't take aspirin or most medicines unless they're prescribed, and even then, I don't usually finish the recommended dosages. I spent most of my childhood, adolescent, and adult years in and out of hospitals, and I got used to the pain. The positive side of me experiencing so many injuries and illnesses is that when something was wrong, I knew it.

In the fall of 2004, I was out doing what I loved to do the most, hitting that little white ball around the golf course. It was warm and I'd been playing by myself, so it was just another normal golf day, other than all the damn balls I lost.

When I got home, I had a slight headache but didn't think much about it. I figured it would go away with a little rest. It took me a little longer to fall asleep that night—my head started feeling worse—but I shrugged it off and counted a few sheep and I was out.

When I woke up my headache had turned into what I believed to be a migraine. Little people were doing construction in my head with a jackhammer on autopilot. My head was throbbing so badly I couldn't keep my eyes open. I even tried aspirin, which I was normally against, but it hurt so bad I was willing to try anything. Aspirin didn't work, so my next move, which I was desperately trying to avoid, was heading to the hospital.

As the pounding in my head got worse and worse, I carefully drove myself to the emergency room of the local hospital that people in the area referred to as "Manslaughter Memorial."

I told the receptionist what was hurting. That, coupled with the pain in my face, was enough to get me looked at immediately. Usually when you go to the emergency room, unless a limb is dangling, your ass is in the waiting room for hours, so I got a little worried when they took me right in.

After an extensive series of tests including a spinal tap, they concluded that I had viral meningitis. I knew by the sound of it that it wasn't good but didn't really know much about it. My first thought was, *is this bad enough that it'll kill me?*

They explained that they needed to admit me. If this went untreated, I could possibly suffer brain or spinal problems. I must've been delusional at that point. All I could think about was when I was going to golf again.

I wasn't about to take any chances, so I informed my family I'd be in the hospital for about a week. Not the kind of call you want to make, especially when I appeared to be fine the day before.

My stay at the hospital wasn't great. One night they brought me a chicken dinner and after one bite I put the tin back over it and left it on the table. The nurse came in before I went to sleep and took the tray out of the room.

I woke up the next morning to a nurse bringing me my breakfast. I propped myself up ready to indulge in some French toast or maybe some waffles. I took the tin off. It was the same chicken from the night before. I kid you not.

The nurse's face said it all. She was as embarrassed as I was disgusted. She closed the tin, apologized, and said she was going to bring me a real breakfast. I told her ass not to bother because I wasn't eating anything from that hospital ever again.

Now I know how they got their nickname.

From that point on I had my family bring me food every day. The damn nurse from the previous night must've placed my tray outside the door where it stayed all night and the day shift nurse, without even checking, returned that same tray back to my table. Trust me, it was a hundred times more revolting than it sounds. That must be what it feels like to be in jail. I bided my time and hoped for early parole.

My week was up, and I was free. Never to set foot back there again. They released me along with my pain medication and I was outie. I wasn't crazy about taking the medication, but for me to relieve some of the pain I didn't have much of a choice.

I made it through the weekend feeling pretty good, so I decided to do some laundry. As I was putting the clothes in the washer my chest started to feel funny and suddenly, I couldn't breathe. My heart was racing, and I was gasping for air. I thought I was going to die.

The next thing I remembered I was lying on the couch in my living room. My wife had called 911 but as I lay there and was able to start breathing normally, I asked her to cancel the paramedics. The last thing I wanted was a spectacle of ambulances and cops in my driveway.

Too late. They all showed up. I was embarrassed. "My God, can these people just leave?" I kept saying to myself, but I knew they wanted me safe.

The EMT I was talking to had a good bedside manner. A young white kid who I could tell wanted what was best for me. He asked me what I did for a living, and I told him I worked for the State Police. I figured that might get him to leave. Not a chance. He was a professional and was determined to make sure I had the best care regardless of my job. I appreciated that. He suggested I go to the hospital to get checked out and asked if I had a preference as to which one. As long as it wasn't the local hospital I didn't care. So off we went, in the ambulance, to Hartford Hospital.

On the way, I explained to the EMT my recent bout with viral meningitis and the medicine that the hospital had prescribed for me. He made a note of all that and asked me what my pain level was from a scale of 0-10, 10 being the worst. I told him that the pain had subsided, so I was close to probably a 2. He told me if I didn't want to be in the emergency room all day then he was going to tell the triage nurse my pain was a 10.

If it was going to get me out of there quicker, he could tell her it was a 15. I didn't care as long as I was in and out. I was frustrated having to be there in the first place. I told the EMT to keep the fact that I was a State Trooper to himself. He agreed.

I arrived at the hospital on a gurney. It was policy, so I went with it. The EMT wheeled me into the triage station through the emergency room and parked me behind this dude, who was also on a gurney, while we waited for the triage nurse to be free. The triage nurse arrived and was talking to the guy on the gurney. Apparently, his catheter had come out. And I thought I had problems.

When she resolved that, they moved him out of the way, and I was next. The EMT talked to the triage nurse.

She was an older white woman with her glasses attached around her neck by a string and balanced on her nose like a tightrope. As they were talking, she looked over at me, shook her head, and removed her glasses. I didn't know why, and I didn't care. I just wanted to be treated so I could go home.

She abruptly stood up from her chair like I was disturbing her morning coffee. She walked over like she was going to scold me. She asked me questions, one of which was my pain level. In my head I was like "Yes, I know this answer. Bob, can I have what is 10 for $100 please?"

I told her what the EMT and I had discussed. She asked if I'd taken any medicine to help with my breathing. I became confused and said, "I didn't know what was wrong so how was I going to take any medicine for it?"

What she said next almost landed her in the hospital. She looked at me and said, "You people think you can come in here and I'm going to give you drugs. Well, not today." She turned to the EMT. "Take him to the waiting room."

It took a few seconds for what she said to sink in. As she walked back to her desk, I could see the faces of the other nurses and the nice EMT who'd helped me out. They were all frozen. No one wanted to move or say anything. They were waiting for me.

When what she said registered, and I saw the look on everyone's face, I lost my everlasting mind. The frustration from being there in the first place, coupled with her comments, set me off to the nth degree, like a shaken soda can that was about to be opened.

"YOU PEOPLE!? BITCH WHO THE FUCK DO YOU THINK YOU'RE TALKING TO!?"

I should have been on a five-second delay.

I tried to jump off the gurney towards her but as luck would have it (for her) I was strapped in. I tried frantically to unstrap myself, but I was so amped up I couldn't find the freakin' button.

The nurse quickly walked back to her station and got on the phone. I don't know who she was calling, but I thought it better be security.

The EMT sprinted over to me and tried his best to calm me down, but it wasn't working. I got off the gurney. The EMT made sure to put himself in between "Nurse Ratched" and me. I wasn't going to touch her, but she didn't know that. She wouldn't even look at me. The last place I wanted to be was there and to have her say that crap to me ignited a week of frustration.

The EMT finally calmed me down and said that he was going to get the "charge nurse," who I guess was her boss, so I could explain to her what happened.

I waited in the foyer. If I'd waited near her station, I would've started up all over again.

The charge nurse finally came and as she walked toward me Nurse Ratched's dumb ass was following right behind her saying she was sorry.

As they both stood in front of me, I told the charge nurse to get her the hell away from me. Nurse Ratched must have known it wasn't a good idea if she stayed so she quickly returned to her station. I tried to explain to the charge nurse what I believed to be racist comments from Nurse Ratched. The charge nurse didn't appear to be interested in what I had to say. She kept cutting me off. By this point I was about to walk out the hospital and go home, but the EMT (bless his soul) convinced me to let them check me out. I agreed and waited by the admitting station.

While I sat there waiting, one of the nurses who was Black and witnessed the whole thing came up to me. She congratulated me for saying something to her. She told me that Nurse Ratched was a racist, and this wasn't the first time she had treated a Black patient unfairly. She went on to say that several of the nurses had warned her about her actions that could one day lead to a patient assaulting her. I felt like that patient. Lucky for her my momma done raised me right.

This nurse got quiet, looked around the room like she was about to do a drug deal with me, and slipped me a piece of paper. It was the name of Nurse Ratched and the name of the director of the hospital. She told me the only way for her to get what's coming to her is if people like me filed complaints. I thanked her for the information, and she parted like the wind.

Moments later, before the charge nurse returned, another nurse who was white, came up to me and reiterated the same thing the Black nurse had told me. I knew at this point I wasn't crazy.

The charge nurse returned, admitted me for a short time, then kicked my ass out. It ended up being a bad reaction to the medicine I was taking for my meningitis.

I headed home and started on the letter. No person, of any color, should be treated like that when they come to a hospital for help. To this day I don't know if she still works there, but if she does it's only a matter a time before she encounters the wrong brotha or sista and they put her ass on a gurney.

I've been asked by many friends if I ever told her I was a State Trooper. My answer was an emphatic "NO!" Me being a trooper had no relevance to the situation. I wanted to be treated as me the patient and not me the trooper. People tend to act differently when they know you're in law enforcement, and I wanted to be treated the way a nurse is supposed to treat a patient: with care and understanding. I got neither.

Chapter 24
PILLOW PETS

Through all the search warrants I've been on and all the busts I've conducted or been a part of, there has been one unfortunate common denominator: kids.

The kids I encountered during undercover buys seemed unbothered by what they were seeing. They appeared in good health, but how long was that going to last? The kids I encountered during search warrants also seemed to be unbothered. It was like they were saying, "I guess the cops are back again."

I was temporarily assigned to a task force in Southern Connecticut where we were executing a search warrant at the house of a drug dealer selling various amounts of crack. We had information that he was home but didn't know what to expect.

We knocked on the front door, stating we were the police and had a search warrant. Usually, you either heard someone answer or you could hear people inside attempting to flee.

This time, nothing.

We used our "universal key," the battering ram, and knocked the door down.

As we made our way through the house it became clear why the dealer hadn't heard us knock, yell, or come in. He was in the back bedroom on the bed with his wife cutting up crack. That wasn't an unusual sight when we executed these warrants. What was unusual—and sickening—was that while they were on the bed cutting up their "product," their infant child was lying on the bed mere feet away from the flying pieces of crack.

When the Department of Children and Families (DCF) gets called to take a child, like in this case, it's never good for anyone. Not for the parent, not for the child, and not for the cop. It's a necessity, but an unfortunate one.

The stress of the job was one thing, but to continually see these kids' lives ruined because of their parents and other influences was a hard thing to deal with. It was just a matter of time before all this pushed me off the edge.

Remember my earlier story about those two generous white NYC police officers who were gracious enough to get this young little Black kid (me) a replacement bike after mine had been stolen? I never forgot it. I knew that someday it would be me who tried to brighten up a kid's day with a gesture they'd never forget. I'd try and pay it forward the best way I knew how.

As a narcotics detective you do countless raids on people's houses and property that usually result in the homeowner getting arrested. When we did these raids, more times than not there were kids present.

As we'd run through these drugs houses screaming, "POLICE WITH A WARRANT!" to secure the residences from any possible threats, I sometimes turned a corner with my gun drawn expecting the worst only to be faced with some innocent young child. This happened way too often and, for me, was the hardest thing to try to get used to. I never did adjust to it.

This never seemed to bother most detectives, but I wasn't like most. I couldn't separate how much I cared about these kids and their well-being, from the job. Others I worked with seemed to be able to put up that wall. I couldn't.

One cold evening in Hartford I'd just given a briefing to the detectives in my squad about a suspect I was targeting who was selling a decent amount of cocaine. The plan was to execute this search warrant on his apartment, seize the drugs, and arrest the target. It sounds easy, but in narcotics you can always count on the unexpected.

We arrived at the perpetrator's apartment building. His car was nowhere in sight. Was he home and we just didn't know? Did his wife take the car? Questions I didn't have the answers to. The only thing I was sure about was that we had a search warrant for his place, and it was going to get served.

I advised my team to set up down the street and I'd keep a look out to see if his car showed up. We waited for almost an hour and nothing. I was like, "The hell with this, let's do the damn thing."

I radioed to our van parked down the street which was filled with detectives wearing body armor and holding battering rams. I told them we weren't going to wait any longer.

We met at the front door of the apartment building and ran up the stairs. As we did, I could feel the tension and nervousness running through all of us that always came with the unexpected when we had to serve a search warrant. Add to this a run up several flights of stairs with our gear on, and all of us were breathing hard as we reached the door.

At the door we did what we always did: Knocked and announced, "POLICE WITH A SEARCH WARRANT!" We waited a few seconds. When the door didn't open, we smashed it in.

One by one we ran cautiously into the apartment, each person covering a corner then moving to a room, all of us going in different directions.

As I entered the apartment, I made a beeline for the living room. That's where I thought the target would be. As I turned into the living room my weapon was pointing at three young children ranging from the ages of about 3 to about 11. They cowered together on the couch, shaking with fear.

I lowered my gun and waited to hear "ALL CLEAR." Once I did, I holstered my weapon, took a deep breath, and approached the three small kids. They were the only people home.

Do you know how heartbreaking that was to find three kids home alone in a supposed drug apartment and here I am with my gun pointed at them like they were kin to Pablo Escobar? It was tough to swallow, but I, as I said, an unfortunate feature of the job.

I knelt down in front of the kids and asked them if they were ok. I assured them that we were not going to hurt them. They knew we were the police, and to them, at that moment, we were the enemy.

I asked them where their daddy and mommy were. None of them knew. That fact alone infuriated me, but I had to remain calm.

Through more conversation with the kids, I was able to call their aunt and have her head over to the apartment.

As we waited for the aunt to arrive, the other detectives searched the apartment and found what we thought we'd find: guns and drugs, both of which could have easily been found by any of the three kids. I was at a boiling point and wanted to do some ungodly things to this guy once I finally got my hands on him.

The aunt arrived. I explained the situation to her. She called the kids' father and coaxed him into coming home with the ruse that one of the kids was sick. Any good parent hears their kid's sick; they're going to come running.

It didn't take long before we heard a key in the door. We hid behind the door and when he took one foot into the apartment it was a wrap. We jumped on his ass like flies on shit.

Once we had him secured, I took him into the bedroom where I talked to him man to man. I told him what we found and how easily his kids could have found it. He first did the stand-up thing by telling me his wife had nothing to do with the guns and drugs. And then like magic he started to cry. As soon as I saw that first tear I was like, "STOP!"

I told him I didn't want to see tears but that he should be upset. I flat out told him if he wanted to kill himself that was between him and God, but his poor kids didn't ask for this and they deserved better. He said he understood and would cooperate with me fully. Whatever happened to him, he'd take his punishment without a fight.

Stand-up guy, huh? Not in my book he wasn't.

The aunt stayed with the children while we cleared the scene.

On the drive home that evening I kept seeing those kids' faces as I stood there with my gun pointed at them. The more I thought about it the worse I felt. I'd come across kids before, but this felt different. I didn't want them to think it was my fault their father wasn't going to be around for a long time, and I sure as hell didn't want them to not trust the police. I had to do something, but what? Then I remembered what those cops in NYC did for me. It was my turn.

The next day I went to the nearest department store and purchased three pillow pets. A pillow pet was this stuffed toy that could be converted from a pillow to a stuffed animal. I thought they were cute and practical. No, I didn't own one.

I headed back to the crime scene. The father was locked up, but I banked on the kids' mother being there. I didn't tell my boss and I didn't tell any of the other detectives what I was about to do. If I had I probably would've been told not to do it, or to forget about it. There were probably hundreds of other reasons I would've been given not to do it, but I'd already made up my mind. When I make up my mind to do something, it's done.

In hindsight I probably should've asked someone to go with me in case something popped off, but I had a feeling everything would be manageable.

I arrived at the apartment and knocked on the door. A lady answered. She was the kids' mother.

Right off the bat she wanted nothing to do with me. Her eyes were rolling, and she had her hands on her hips as if to say, "You have five seconds to get the hell out of my face." I explained that I was there to try and change her kids' opinion of the police and wanted her permission to let me give the pillow pets to her daughters.

"No," she said.

She told me she'd give the pillow pets to the kids. Sure, sell me a bridge while you're at it. I knew the message I wanted to say to the kids would not be relayed. And if it was, it wouldn't be the way I wanted it. In that moment, my mission of spreading a little good news about the police was a lost cause.

I left there in good spirits. At least I tried to do the right thing.

As for the drug-dealing father, I buried him in court. He ended up getting sent to prison for a long time, which meant he was not abusing his kids by dealing drugs in front of them or leaving them alone every minute he was out conducting his "business." That was good enough for me.

As a police officer it's not always about how many tickets you give or about how many search warrants you execute, sometimes it's about how many lives you've changed and will they be better for meeting you on that day. Deep down I felt the mother of those three kids knew I was trying to do the right thing, but she couldn't let that show because, I believed, she would have thought doing so would've made her appear weak.

I continued in my unit for a while longer, but this case would be one of the last I'd conduct. For me, dealing with race was one thing. but kids made the job that much harder.

As a police officer there's always a case that sticks with you for the rest of your life. For me, this was it. I tried to put those girls in the back of my mind, but the harder I tried the more I thought about them. It was time for me to stop concentrating on these kids before it got to the point where I might make a mistake and take out my frustrations on one of the parents. This was the case that tipped the scales toward my retirement. I couldn't take it anymore. My time as a narcotics detective/state trooper was coming to an end. It was time for me to be completely done.

Some months after the aforementioned search warrant, while sitting at an office meeting, a feeling came over me and I realized right then and there it was time for me to put in my retirement papers. Those three kids, along with the many years of police work, weighed heavily on my mind when I made my decision. I texted my wife with a straightforward message – "I'm done". We later discussed it and agreed it was the right decision.

Chapter 25
HELP ME

There were a lot of things in my life that were instrumental in my development as a man, a father, and a State Trooper. So many things changed the way I thought about people and myself, but the story I'm about to tell had the biggest impact on my life and would change me forever. It happened early in my career as a trooper. I went back and forth on whether to share this story, but after a long discussion with my beautiful daughter, she helped me realize that this was a big part of who I am. I saved it for the end because it was the hardest to tell. I can count on one hand the number of people outside of my family I've shared this story with. Now it's time I share it with you.

It was early spring of 1992. I'd been a State Trooper for about two years and was still learning the ropes. We had an abnormal schedule where we'd work five days on and three days off, so my "weekends" would occasionally fall during the week.

When my days off came at that time in my life, I'd usually spend them with friends. Maybe hitting up a club, taking in a movie, or just downright chillin. One thing I wouldn't do is talk about anything relating to police work. If I did mention it at all, it was with my parents. They always wanted to know how it was going and would worry about me, and rightfully so.

I'd usually wait until my days off rolled around before I'd call them. It would give me a chance to gather my wits from the stress that built up during my workweek. I talked to my mother more often than I did my father. I guess I was a bit of a momma's boy. When people used to tease me and tell me I was spoiled, she'd quickly say I wasn't spoiled, I was loved.

This particular weekend I decided to hit up my dad. It had been a while since we'd chopped it up. When we did talk it was always about me. I'd ask him about how he was doing and all he'd say is, "I'm good! Everything is everything."

I got myself settled on my couch in anticipation of a lengthy catch-up conversation with Pops. We both could talk, so I had to be comfortable.

I grabbed the phone and dialed his number. As the phone rang, I was trying to remember all the crazy things that had happened at work that I wanted to tell him. A few rings went by before the phone was answered. The voice on the other end said, "Hello?"

It was a male voice I didn't recognize.

My dad lived alone, so hearing another person's voice caught me off guard and made me concerned. It could've been a friend stopping by, so I didn't jump to any conclusions.

"Who's this?" I asked.

With straight up arrogance the guy responded, "You called here. Who are you?"

I went from 0-60 in a snap of the fingers. The blood in my veins started pumping to a beat I wasn't used to. You don't answer the phone that way at someone else's home.

I didn't say what I wanted to. My only concern was getting my father on the phone so I could tell him that whoever his boy was he needed to be checked.

"This is Matt. Again, who are you?"

He told me his name but at that point I didn't remember, nor did I care.

"Oh, you're Barney's son," he said.

Barney was my dad's nickname as far back as I could remember. The man told me to hold on, and that he'd get him. As I sat there pissed at some asshole on the phone, I wanted to vent to my father about him before we got into our normal conversation.

The guy on the phone said, "Here he is."

"Hey Pop, who was—?" I didn't get to finish my sentence.

My father interrupted me with the most quiet and scared voice I'd ever heard. "Help me. Please help me."

The first thing I said to myself was, *Holy shit I'm going to kill someone today!* That's the way I felt, but whoever answered that phone had something to do with why my father had said those words. As angry as I was, I was also scared. I didn't know what to do.

I gathered myself the best I could and said, "Dad, what's wrong?"

He responded the same way he did when he answered the phone. "Help me, please."

"Hang in there, I'm on my way."

I jumped up off the couch, got dressed, and hopped in my car to head to New York.

At the speeds I was hitting, it felt like my car was flying. Every time I hit a bump or a dip in the road my car felt as if it were airborne. They taught me in the police academy that when you're responding to an accident or a crime scene, you're no good to anybody if you don't get there safely. I didn't give a shit. I was getting there as quickly as possible. This was about family.

As I sped toward the city my head started to spin. I didn't know what to expect when I got there. My eyes started to get a little watery, but I had to compose myself. Trying to drive safely with watery eyes is damn near impossible. I was scared for him. I was scared for what I might have to do when I arrived.

There are lots of people who'll tell you what they'd do in a given situation. I didn't know what I'd do and that scared me. As I got closer my hands started to shake. Once I got there, I'd have to handle business.

I arrived in Harlem onto Riverside Drive by New York Presbyterian Hospital. The minute I did my car started to slow down. The reality hit me—this situation could go terribly bad.

I made sure my mind was clear. I needed to make sound, rational decisions.

I pulled up in front of his apartment building, took a deep breath, and walked to the front of the building. I buzzed my dad's apartment.

The same asshole answered. "Who?"

"It's Matt. Buzz me in." I had a little of my own arrogance going on.

I rode in the elevator to my dad's top-floor apartment, all the while thinking about what I was going to find inside.

The elevator came to a stop, and I exited. *This is going to be the last time.* I didn't know for what or for whom, or even why.

My hand was shaking as I rang the doorbell. The person inside got closer. The bolts behind the door unlocked and the door opened.

There he was, the asshole on the phone.

My first inclination was to lay him out, but my father took precedence. I shoved him out of my way and made a beeline to my father's bedroom.

What I found started to make me cry.

The man who made me the man I am today, who taught me how to drive and how to handle myself, lay in his bed motionless, his body withered away to almost nothing. His speech was almost unrecognizable. There were tears in his eyes.

He reached his arms out to me and said, "Help me."

I wiped away my own tears. "You're safe now. I got you."

I took a second, then turned toward the asshole. "What did you do to him!?"

He nonchalantly said, "I didn't do anything to him. He has AIDS."

I lunged at him and grabbed him by the collar. "You have three seconds to leave this apartment or you're not leaving at all."

While still in my grasp he said, "I'm not going anywhere. I live here."

"The fuck you do!" My grip was getting tighter, so I released him.

He stood there for a second. "I'll leave, but I'll be back." He grabbed his coat and walked out the door.

I locked the door behind him, rushed back, and knelt by my father's bedside. I told him I was sorry. Sorry it happened, sorry for the asshole, and sorry I hadn't been there for him.

For the first time, I had no idea what to do. The only person he had to depend on was me. My sister was living on the other side of the country and my mom and him were divorced.

My dad had always struggled with alcohol; it was a big reason for my parents' divorce. I'd become aware of his progression to drugs when I was in college, but I had no idea things were this bad. It made me mad. I should've been there to help him, and I wasn't. Now I'd have to live with this pain for the rest of my life, and whatever time he had left. He was dying right before my eyes. I refused to let him die alone. I refused to let him die with that asshole.

I stayed with him for a while, then I told him I had to go but that I'd be back when I figured out what to do. I grabbed his house key and headed to my mom's place.

When I got there, I explained what I'd just seen.

Even though they were divorced, she didn't wish this on him. But she felt worse for me. She knew I'd have to carry this burden alone.

My mom and I discussed potential options, but I had to make the final decision. The minute I walked through his door I expected my life would change, but never in the way it did.

I kissed and hugged my mother goodbye and thanked her for her guidance. Her compassion is second to none. After talking to her I had the strength to do what was necessary to care for my father.

I went to my father's apartment and told him I had to head back to Connecticut. I needed clothes and other essentials. I told him that when I returned, I wasn't leaving his side until he was safe.

He mustered a smile and said, "I love you."

I didn't want him to see me break down in tears again so I told him I loved him and said I'd be back as soon as I could.

I got back in my car. This was only the beginning. That asshole and I would have to encounter each other again. Next time things would end up being different. I hoped it wouldn't involve any physical confrontation. If it did, he was going to lose.

After a few days of heavy thought and prayer I packed a bag and got ready to head back to the city. Again, I'm not the most religious person in the world. I don't go to church, but I do believe in God. That day I prayed like I never have before for the strength to get me through the day. It was going to be a trying day, me having to deal with my dad's condition and his so-called roommate. I needed all the strength I could muster.

I called my mom and told her I'd be heading to my dad's. I wanted her to know in case something happened to me. I know she was worried. I was, too.

Black Behind the Shield

    My drive to New York was slower this time. I was preoccupied with the scenarios I could encounter when I got to my dad's apartment. I went over 100 of them. But it's always the 101st that you don't account for.
    I was about five blocks away, and as each block went by my heart started to race quicker and quicker. I was ready. I had a better understanding of what I was dealing with. One thing was for sure: I wasn't leaving there without him.
    I parked on the hill just past the entrance to his building. I took a deep breath and slowly got out of the car.
    When you're a cop, the first thing that's imbedded in you is to know what and who's around you. I scanned up and down the block like I was looking for Bin Laden. Everything looked clear. I walked down the hill toward the entrance.
    As I was making my way a guy was walking up the hill toward me. Maybe it was the cop in me, but something didn't strike me as right about him. He was walking at a brisk pace, he kept looking over his shoulder, and he was carrying a small paper bag. The indications were of someone hiding something or who was about to do something. I slowed. I wanted to make sure when he walked by me there was no drama.
    We were about ten feet from each other when he took a sharp turn into the walkway of my father's building and headed toward the buzzers. He nodded as he walked in front of me. I reciprocated with a quick nod of my own. I walked behind him and as I pulled out my dad's apartment keys the man buzzed my father's apartment.

He was a crackhead. He was either bringing drugs upstairs or he was meeting people who already had some inside. Either way, he wasn't going to get the chance.

I put my keys away and waited for him to get buzzed in. The same asshole that answered when I'd come before answered when this guy rang. There were at least two people now that I had to deal with.

Normally I would've been nervous, but with the adrenaline that was pumping inside me, I could have taken on ten people.

The door buzzed and I walked into the building right behind him, my eyes glued to the back of his head, which I'm sure he could feel. We both stood waiting for the elevator to arrive with my eyes still glued to his dome. He started to get a little fidgety, probably because I wouldn't stop staring at him.

He gave me a double take before entering the elevator. The elevator was the size of most people's closet, so we were close. I could tell in his eyes he realized who the hell I was. My picture was all over my dad's apartment. If he knew who I was, he knew what my occupation was.

As he pushed the button for the top floor his hands were shaking. I moved closer and closer to him. I was so close I could practically count the molecules in every bead of sweat that started to roll down his brow.

"So, you're on your way to see Barney, huh?" I said.

All he could muster was, "Uh, yeah."

"Good. Me too."

The elevator came to a stop at the top floor. I was going to do something, but neither one of us knew what.

We both exited the elevator with me bringing up the rear. It was about 10 feet from the elevator to my dad's door. He knocked on the door and as he did, I stepped to the side so that asshole wouldn't see me through the peephole. The bolts and locks started to get undone. My adrenaline was so intense my breathing could probably be heard down the hall.

The door opened and the guy from the elevator yelled at the top of his lungs, "BARNEY'S SON IS HERE, BARNEY'S SON IS HERE!"

That adrenaline that I keep mentioning turned into what they call superhuman strength. I grabbed the guy from the elevator, picked him up and threw him in the air into the closed door of the elevator. His feet never touched the ground.

I reached in and grabbed Mr. Asshole and he got the same treatment. He had no smart comments or statements because he could see the rage in my eyes. I knew there were other people in the apartment, I just didn't know how many, where they were and whether they were armed. It wasn't a big apartment so the only other places they could be were in the living room or the back room.

I ran into the apartment like I'd lost my mind. As I did, I passed my father's bedroom. He lay there, still bedridden. I didn't say anything to him as I passed because I was focused on what I was about to encounter.

I guess the guy from the elevator didn't yell loud enough. As I turned the corner into my old bedroom, I saw three guys huddled around a makeshift table made of cardboard where they were all smoking crack.

I took a moment to assess each person and to see if I could observe any weapons. As I was looking at them, they were looking at each other as if to say, "So what the hell are we gonna do?"

The rage in me continued. I threw my jacket off, ready for an all-out brawl. I didn't care that there were three of them. They were all going to leave one way or the other.

I grabbed the neck of the guy closest to me. The others had seen enough already. They jumped over him and ran out of the apartment.

The guy in my grip was struggling to breathe. I released him before he went unconscious and allowed him to run out as well. I ran to the door and made sure they were all gone. Then I locked the door behind them.

I returned to my dad's bedside and said, "Don't worry Pop. I'm not leaving you again."

With no strength left in his body he reached out and hugged me.

In that moment, I couldn't be strong anymore. I broke down and cried in his arms. I didn't want to let go of him. I didn't know how much longer he was going to be with me.

I took a deep breath and gathered myself. We still weren't safe yet. I didn't know if those guys were going to come back and, if so, with what or with whom. I told my dad I was going to take him to the hospital to see if they could help him.

I grabbed some clothes and got him dressed. I put some extra clothes in a bag. I knew he couldn't come back home.

Black Behind the Shield

    We left for the first hospital and after waiting about five hours they told me that there was nothing they could do for him because he was going to die anyway, and they weren't going to admit him just to give him medicine to make him feel better. Are you effing kidding me!?

    The next hospital I took him to said pretty much the same thing. My third try was St. Luke's Hospital on Amsterdam Avenue. This time I was playing my cop card. I told them I was a State Trooper from Connecticut and that I needed their help. I explained briefly what happened and what his supposed condition was.

    They tested him and like the other two hospitals, confirmed that he had AIDS. They also broke it down to me that he didn't have long to live, but that they would admit him and keep him comfortable until he passed.

    I had never been more grateful than I was for their generosity. At least he wouldn't die in his bed alongside a bunch of crackheads.

    Once I knew he was comfortable and secure I went out to my car and sat for a while blaming myself for the things that happened, even though they weren't my fault. I left but would return on all my days off to spend with him.

    When I did visit him, I'd talk, and he'd listen. He really couldn't speak much anymore. He'd give me an occasional smile that I'll never forget. I even showed up in my uniform one day because he had never seen me in it before. He was as proud of me as I was of him.

    I went to see him each day I could get off, week after week, as he died a little more. The time was near, and I braced myself for the reality of him leaving me.

Then it happened. I got that dreaded phone call that he had passed. Even though it hurt, I was okay with it. He wasn't suffering anymore.

I might be in the minority, but I believe everything happens for a reason. This entire ordeal helped me grow not only as a person but also as a State Trooper. It helped me understand how to react in the most stressful of situations. To analyze the moment and prioritize what my options are. It taught me that life is precious and shouldn't be snuffed out just because you're angry. Those guys were doing drugs just like my dad was. If I'd taken one of them out, would that have made my dad any different? Yes, I was furious. I felt I'd let him down, that I wasn't there when he needed me, but I made sure I was with him when he needed me the most. He'll always be remembered, and never forgotten. Love you Pop!

Chapter 26
MY TESTIMONY

I loved the shield, I respected the shield, I honored the shield, and I will never regret serving the shield. But we as police officers must do a better job policing ourselves before we can police others. I learned that while I was on the job, but it became clearer once I retired. Sometimes emotions get the best of us. We're human. That's understandable. It happened to me, but I always thought about that other option. If I reacted to every emotion while I was on the job, I'd be writing this book from a not-so-comfortable place.

It's a fine line between enforcing the law and thinking you *are* the law. As a police officer, like it or not, you are by default held to a higher standard than most. It's not an easy job. In fact, it's one of the most difficult and demanding jobs in America, but we chose to do it, and with it comes great responsibility.

My old weapons instructor used to say it's easy to pull the trigger but it's hard as hell to deal with where that bullet ends up. That also applies to the things people say. It's easy to call someone a nigger, but would that same person do it if they were by themselves with no backup talking to three Black guys? I think not. Take a moment to think about what you say and do before you say or do it.

Matthew Barnwell III

I took this job because I wanted to help people. That may sound like a cliché but it's the truth. There are those who don't want to be helped, and that's fine. But as police officers it's not our job to condemn them. Our job is to try to understand them. You can't please everyone, but if you please one, we're moving in the right direction.

We took an oath to serve and protect the community and by all accounts we're failing. We must realize that when the cop next to us messes up, we all do. As police officers we don't have the luxury of saying, "It wasn't me." We have to take responsibility not only for our actions, but the actions of our fellow officers. Everyone must be held accountable.

We have to stop profiling the Black community. We can't assume people of color are guilty before proven innocent. Way too many Black and brown people are ending up severely injured or dead simply because of what they look like, and for that there's no excuse. It's one thing for a racist police officer to treat Blacks within his or her own department badly (which shouldn't be the case), but when that same racist police officer unleashes that hatred towards people in the community, it should never be accepted or tolerated. I had to deal with racism from the very people who swore to uphold the law. It made me a stronger and more thick-skinned human being.

Finally, to the citizens these brave men and women try to protect, please be patient. These officers have a difficult job to do, and they'll make mistakes, just as you would. It's easy to "Monday morning quarterback" an officer's decision from the comforts of your own home.

Black Behind the Shield

In the media cops always seem to be in the wrong, so I know what I'm about to say is hard, but let's get all the facts before we condemn them. There are so many good, hard-working, and compassionate men and women who wear the shield, and every day they try to have a positive impact within the community. Unfortunately, those same police officers get overshadowed by the few who use their shield as a weapon.

When a person becomes combative and argumentative right off the rip, it puts a police officer on the defensive. Just as we expect police officers to take a minute before they react, they need the public to do the same for them.

I dedicated over 24 years of my life to the Connecticut State Police, and it was nothing less than amazing. It is, in my opinion, the best police agency in America. I met a lot of great people who taught me a lot of great things and for that I'll always be grateful. Of course, with every job you have your ups and downs, and I used both to help me grow as a person. I was fortunate enough to retire young and healthy, and I plan to continue pursuing those things that escaped my grasp when I was younger. I still can't sing, but maybe the big screen is next. As our motto from my State Police graduating class read, "WALK WITH PRIDE."

Chapter 27
Epilogue: I'VE BEEN...

I've been... judged for the color of my skin.

I've been... in an elevator with a white woman who clenches her purse with all her might in fear that I might steal it.

I've been... pulled over for Driving while Black.

I've been... followed around a store by security for no reason.

I've been... called a nigger by a white person.

I've been... ignored by a waitress who didn't want to serve me because I was Black.

I've been... walking down a street in the middle of the day only to have a white woman look at me, grab her purse, and cross the street to avoid me.

I've been... called "good boy" by a superior, while on duty and twice on the golf course.

I've been... on a plane where a white woman decided not to sit next to me even though that was the only open seat available within five rows of me.

I've been... asked if I carry a gun or have been stabbed because I mentioned I was from Harlem.

I've been... in several situations where a gun has been pointed at me because I was Black.

I've been... told I don't sound Black because I'm well spoken.

I've been... able to avoid confrontations because I am well spoken.

I've been... at a police call only to have the door slammed in my face because the homeowner didn't believe I was a cop because I was Black.

I've been... spit at by a white person.

I've been... accused of sexual misconduct because I was Black.

I've been... a good son, brother, father, and husband.

I've been... able to defy societal beliefs and make it out of the hood and become an asset to society.

I've been... willing to stand up for what I believe is right even if other people don't agree.

I've been... a volunteer with my daughter to pick up garbage at a beach for no other reason than it was the right thing to do.

I've been... able to teach my son how to be a proud Black man.

I've been... at a gas station gassing up my shiny BMW 535i when a white guy asked me, "How did you get that car"? Not "Where?" or "When?", not even "Why?", but "HOW."

I've been... a man who still believes in racial equality.

I've been... a man who believes that it's not the color of your skin that defines you but how you treat others.

I've been... taught not to hate.

I've been... taught that you're not born a racist: it's something learned.

Matthew Barnwell III

    I've been... trying to count the days where you don't see or hear something racist. (I CAN'T!)
    I've been... under the belief that if you're not Black you can't pretend to understand what we've gone through, and still go through, every day.
    I've been a lot of things, but what I've been most proud of being is a BLACK MAN IN AMERICA!

Chapter 28
TRIBUTE

I thought it would be important to never forget those Black men and women who lost their lives to police brutality or racial violence. George Floyd's life was snuffed out because an overzealous white police officer without conscience kept his knee on Mr. Floyd's neck for 8 minutes and 46 seconds. Some will argue the amount of time, but any amount of time was too much, especially with multiple police officers surrounding one person who was on the ground handcuffed.

Breonna Taylor was gunned down during an apparent no-knock drug search warrant. The boyfriend thought the police were intruders and fired upon them. In my 20 years in the narcotics unit and serving hundreds of search warrants, we always announced our intentions when knocking on the door prior to executing a search warrant, specifically for that reason. We wanted the homeowners to know it was the police forcing entry into their home and not an intruder.

Then there was the youngster, Trayvon Martin. He was fatally shot by a white neighborhood watch member, George Zimmerman, in Sanford, Florida. Martin had left his house to buy skittles and an iced tea but was deemed suspicious by Zimmerman, and when Martin ran because Zimmerman was following him, he was shot. Even though Zimmerman wasn't a police officer he decided to take the law into his own hands and kill an innocent young Black man.

And to Ahmaud Arbery, Tamir Rice, Philando Castile, Alton Sterling and the countless other Black men and women who've been killed due to police and racial violence, you will never be forgotten. Nor will those whose deaths that went unreported and didn't get the press they deserved.

This could be any of us at any time. Black people live with that fear every day. It's not something a white person will ever understand no matter how hard they try, but it's real. Until racism is wiped from the face of the earth, that fear will remain within us.

I've been asked on a few occasions what made me write this book. It goes back to a walk I was taking while on the phone with my mom. When I told her I was on a walk, the first thing she said was, "Be careful." This was soon after the murder of George Floyd, so race tensions were high. Her "Be careful" had a different tone to it than normal. I told her not to worry, I was walking in my neighborhood. As soon as I said that I realized that's probably what Ahmaud Arbery was thinking when he went out for his run. My walk went from casual to "I better keep my head on a swivel."

No one should feel they can't enjoy the breeze on their face while taking a stroll without fearing the cops or some racist is going to approach them and do Lord knows what.

I wrote this book because first, I wanted my children to know what I went through growing up and how I got to where I am amidst all the racism I faced.

Black Behind the Shield

There are people who faced much, much more, but to me what I faced was a lot.

Second, it was good for me to vent, to make myself feel I wasn't alone in this fight. I'd get frustrated listening to and seeing all the violence against people of color and for me, writing helped soothe that frustration, even if only for a moment.

Third, I wanted to be heard, and to make it clear that, yes, I was a Black police officer, and I did face racism, but that there are so many good people out there—white, Black, you name it. Also, that police officers are good people. Most of them joined their respective police departments to do good. The ones who didn't, those are the ones we should be trying to get rid of. If we don't, nothing will change.

In today's world we see countless ways in which people want to be heard pertaining to racial injustice and police brutality. Mine was writing. Others speak out by peacefully protesting. It's something that's been around forever but continues to be labeled as "outrageous." Speaking for myself, it appears that many of these peaceful protests turn into violent demonstrations because people in political power deem them threatening and use excessive tactics to stop them. If I'm trying to talk and you keep putting your hand over my mouth, we're going to have a problem that could turn physical.

Protests are a way of publicly making your opinions heard.

I condone, and support, protests. I don't condone riots, but I can understand why they happen. However, the looters during these riots are nothing more than opportunists using unfortunate situations (like George Floyd's death) to wreak havoc on those innocent members of the community who open their stores to serve the same people who are looting them.

Speaking as a former member of law enforcement, being on the front lines during a protest is no easy task. Sometimes you get spit at, yelled at, and called every name in the book, and you have to stand there and take it. I understand that people blame the police for many of the things going on today—and they should, I do as well—but I'll say it again, not all cops are bad. It's tough for me. I feel as though I'm in the middle of both sides. Cops need to do much better and the public has to understand the actions of a few are not indicative of the actions of most.

Instead of taking money away from the police, why don't we spend that money on more extensive training so that police officers learn to better handle community-based issues such as race and mental health? People need to trust that we as police officers will be able to handle a traffic stop, execute a search warrant, or simply conduct an officer/civilian interaction without prejudice or bias. Without proper training and the weeding out of the "bad apples," it'll never happen.

I pray that one day we won't have to protest for racial justice and against police brutality because everyone will be treated the same. It seems that every time we take a step in the right direction, we take two steps back. With that as our path we'll never get ahead. But if we as a society keep trying, listening, and addressing those hard to talk about issues I think we can.

Black Behind the Shield

For all you brothas and sistas out there, remain strong. Who you are is enough!

ACKNOWLEDGEMENTS

    First and foremost, I'd like to thank you mom. Without you, there is no me. Everything that I do and have become is because of you. You've always put me in a position to succeed. Whether it be physically, emotionally, or mentally. Words are not enough but these words are forever. I love you!

    To my sister-thank you for always having my back and believing in me. You've been my biggest supporter since we were kids and it's that support that allows me to believe in myself. Thanks Mush!

    To my family-thank you for always being there when I need you. This book was written because of you guys. Y'all made it easy for me. You pushed me to be a better writer and made me a better person. Also, thanks to my dog Roxy for listening to me when I would get frustrated even if you didn't want to.

    Thanks to my very dear friend Erica (Swerve). We've been friends for a minute and it's that friendship and candor that helped point out ways to make my book better. I'll never forget that, and I will never forget you.

    My cousin Raymond-thank you for taking the time to read one of my drafts and giving me your honest feedback. Your input was vital in the progress of this book. Love ya' cuz'!

Black Behind the Shield

To Greg Elliot-thank you for editing this book and putting the gloss on it that it needed. Your mind is truly one of a kind.

Author Amber Mosely-even though we just met you took time from your busy schedule to guide me through the publishing process and answer any question I had. I really appreciate that. Thank you.

To my boy Chan Booth Esq.-thank you brah for the hours on top of hours we spent going over this book to make sure everything was on point. Your friendship has truly meant the world to me.

To Erin Ortega-I could not have found a better person to design my cover. Not only are you a very talented artist and graphic designer but you're even a better person. I'm truly honored that you took time away from your busy life to collaborate with me. Words will never begin to express my gratitude! Thank you so very much!

To my relatives, friends (near and far) and to my extended family-thank you for all the words of encouragement not just during this process but throughout my life. I appreciate all of you.

To all my peeps in NYC-thank you all for being genuine and staying true to yourselves. You made growing up in the city the best part of my life. ("Matty yessss")

To my very dear friend David Pesci-Wow! I really don't know how to say thank you enough. You helped me from the beginning. The tons of emails, texts, and edits that you were subjected to were answered and completed without any hesitation. If it weren't for your expertise, diligence, and willingness to help me, this book would never have been completed. Facts! I am humbled and thankful to call you my friend.

And to YOU, the reader, thank you for purchasing my book. It's my hope that you were able to gain some insight into my life and be able to use what you learned for your own personal growth.

Made in the USA
Middletown, DE
01 February 2024